THE JOURNAL OF THE BLACK CATHOLIC THEOLOGICAL SYMPOSIUM (BCTS), was founded in 2007.

MANUSCRIPTS should be submitted to the editorial board by the deadline announced at the Annual Meeting, which is also posted at http://www.bcts.org. All submissions must be formatted in Chicago Turabian style with Works Cited page and sent via electronic mail to senior editor Kimberly Flint-Hamilton: kflintha@stetson.edu, and also to editor Cecilia Moore: Cecilia.Moore@notes.udayton.edu. For examples of Chicago Turabian style, see: http://www.lib.berkeley.edu/instruct/guides/chicago-turabianstyle.pdf

Contributors must submit original work. The Journal of the Black Catholic Theological Symposium is composed of original articles by its members, and will not publish manuscripts that have been previously published elsewhere.

REVIEWS of books or films that have relevance to the Black Catholic Theological Symposium may also be submitted and will be considered for publication. Reviews originally published elsewhere will not be considered for publication.

MEMBERSHIP in the Black Catholic Theological Symposium is by invitation only. Those interested in joining the organization may review membership guidelines from Article II of the Constitution, posted on the BCTS web site: http://www.bcts.org, and contact the secretary of the BCTS, Shawnee Daniels-Sykes, SSND, at the following electronic mail address: sykess@mtmary.edu.

The opinions expressed in the articles and/or reviews published in the Journal of the Black Catholic Theological Symposium are those of the authors and are not necessarily the opinions of the editorial board, the organization, or the publisher.

The Journal of the Black Catholic Theological Symposium is provided to all paid members of the BCTS. Additional copies of the journal may be obtained by contacting the publisher, Steven Hamilton, of Fortuity Press, at the following electronic mail address: steven.hamilton@fortuitypress.com.

Fortuity Press
Copyright © 2010 by Fortuity Press LLC
All rights reserved.

No part of this volume may be reprinted or reproduced or utilized in any form by any electronic, mechanical, or other means, now known or hereafter invented, including photocopying and recording, or any information storage or retrieval system, without permission in writing from the publishers.

Printed in the United States of America.
Cover design by Kimberly Flint-Hamilton, Steven Hamilton
Interior design by Kimberly Flint-Hamilton, Steven Hamilton

The editors wish to express heartfelt gratitude to poet Mari Evans for granting permission to print an excerpt from her poem, "Speak The Truth To The People," which appears in its entirety in her wonderful collection: *Continuum: New and Selected Poems*
(Baltimore, MD: Black Classic Press, 1970).

THE JOURNAL
OF THE
BLACK CATHOLIC THEOLOGICAL SYMPOSIUM (BCTS) VOLUME FOUR

EDITORS

Cyprian Davis, O.S.B., Editor-in-Chief
Saint Meinrad Archabbey

Kimberly Flint-Hamilton, Senior Editor
Stetson University

Cecilia Moore, Editor
University of Dayton

CONSULTANTS
Sue Houchins, Bates College
Jamie T. Phelps, O.P., Xavier University
C. Vanessa White, Catholic Theological Union

THE BLACK CATHOLIC THEOLOGICAL SYMPOSIUM (BCTS)

2010 OFFICERS

Bryan Massingale, Convener
C. Vanessa White, Associate Convener
Shawnee Daniels-Sykes, S.S.N.D., Secretary
Robert Bartlett, Treasurer
Cyprian Davis, O.S.B., Archivist
Kimberly Flint-Hamilton, Past Convener

THE JOURNAL OF THE BCTS

Volume Four   October 2010

LETTER FROM THE EDITORS

Kimberly Flint-Hamilton   1
A Year of Commemorations

ESSAYS

Thea Bowman, F.S.P.A., Ph.D. (1937-1990)

   Cyprian Davis, O.S.B.   3
   I Knew Sister Thea Bowman

   Maurice J. Nutt, C.Ss.R.   5
   Thea Bowman: The Courage To Keep On Keeping On!

Thirty Years and Counting: The Institute for Black
Catholic Studies – 1980-2010

   Kathleen Dorsey Bellow   13
   A Thirty Year Collaboration in Uniquely Black and
   Catholic Mission

   C. Vanessa White   17
   Thirty Years of Impact: The Institute for
   Black Catholic Studies

ARCHIVAL PROJECT

Christopher J. Kauffman   21
Cyprian Davis's Contributions to the Study of
African American Catholic History:
Articles in the *U.S. Catholic Historian*

Cecilia Moore and Kimberly Flint-Hamilton   29
Cyprian Davis, O.S.B.: To Walk a Path,
To Be Transformed, And To Transform

ARTICLES

M. Shawn Copeland 57
The Role of the Black Catholic Theologian and
Scholar in Today's Context

Diane Batts Morrow 81
"Righteous Discontent:" Black Catholic Protest in the
United States of America, 1817-1941

Nathaniel Holmes, Jr. 97
Redemptive Suffering and Christology in
African American Christian Theology

Kwame Assenyoh, S.V.D. 121
The Decline of Black Catholicism:
What's Racial Slavery To Do With It?

BOOK REVIEWS

Charlene Smith, F.S.P.S. and John Feister, 147
Thea's Song: The Life of Thea Bowman (D. Hayes)

Bryan Massingale, *Racial Justice and the* 150
Catholic Church (S. Peppers-Bates)

M. Shawn Copeland, *Enfleshing Freedom: Body,* 156
Race, and Being (K. Flint-Hamilton)

A Year Of Commemorations

Kimberly Flint-Hamilton, Senior Editor
Stetson University

The year 2010 is a very special one for the BCTS. This year we commemorate a number of very significant events, all of which have contributed to making our organization what it is today.

Thirty years ago, in 1980, The Institute for Black Catholic Studies (IBCS) first opened its doors. Born out of the passion of the National Black Catholic Clergy Caucus and refined during that first meeting of the BCTS in 1978, the IBCS has been instrumental in the formation of adults committed to an authentically Black and Catholic ministry. The Institute has produced dozens of Masters in Theology, several of whom have gone on to earn doctorates in Theology. Who can say how many lives have been enriched by the Institute? Upon completion of their certification programs and Masters Degrees, students return to their communities with a renewed appreciation for and understanding of the Word of God and the needs of the Black Catholic community. Thousands may already have been touched by the Institute. Kathleen Dorsey Bellow and C. Vanessa White reflect on the Institute's thirty years of ministry.

Sadly, just ten years following the opening of the IBCS's programs, we lost one of its founders, Sr. Dr. Thea Bowman, F.S.P.A.. Sr. Thea's vision illuminated the paths of many. We celebrate life of this remarkable woman who inspired so many people by commemorating the twentieth anniversary of her passing with reflections by Cyprian Davis O.S.B. and Maurice J. Nutt, C.Ss. R.

This year the Journal launches a new initiative. The Journal's *Archival Project* is dedicated to preserving the histories of our senior members by a day or two of interviews, followed by an essay in the Journal that summarizes the highlights of our colleagues' accomplishments, inspirations, and experiences. In this year's Journal we begin the *Archival Project* with our first essay which celebrates the life of one of our founding members, Dom. Cyprian Davis, O.S.B. – a fitting start as Fr. Cyprian celebrated his 80th birthday on September 9, 2010! We hope to continue the *Archival Project* with an essay published in the Journal every year. Additionally, a tribute to Fr. Cyprian and his contributions to Black Catholic scholarship are offered by guest contributor Christopher J. Kauffman, editor of *U.S. Catholic Historian*. Kauffman dedicated the Winter issue of *U.S.C.H.* Volume 28 (2010) to Fr. Cyprian and his groundbreaking work.

This year's articles include M. Shawn Copeland's paper reflecting on 40 years of black theological scholarship (*The Role of the Black Catholic Theologian and Scholar in Today's Context*), Diane Batts Morrow's article on the agency shown by black Catholics in their parishes between the years 1817 and 1941 (*"Righteous Discontent:" Black Catholic Protest in the United States of American, 1817-1941*), Nathaniel Holmes' paper engaging the debate on the redemptive nature of suffering in African American religious thought (*Redemptive Suffering and Christology in African American Christian Theology*), and Kwame Assenyoh's analysis of racism in the Catholic Church and its role in the current decline of Black Catholicism (*The Decline of Black Catholicism: What's Racial Slavery To Do With It?*). We also review three books: *Racial Justice and the Catholic Church* by our convener, Bryan Massingale; *Enfleshing Freedom: Body, Race, and Being* by founding member and former convener M. Shawn Copeland; and, in honor of Sr. Thea Bowman, F.S.P.A. *Thea's Song: The Life of Thea Bowman* by Charlene Smith, F.S.P.A. and John Feister.

Volume 4 of the Journal of the BCTS continues to break new ground and promises to engage and stimulate. You won't be able to put it down!

Thea Bowman, F.S.P.A., Ph.D. (1937-1990)

The year 2010 marks another anniversary, this one more somber than the others. Sister Thea Bowman, F.S.P.A., Ph.D., after a great deal of suffering, finally lost her battle to cancer in 1990. Her zest for living, her profound spirituality, and her joy marked all those who had the honor of knowing her. Here are two reflections on her life and influence, the first by Cyprian Davis, O.S.B. who worked with Sr. Thea at the Institute for Black Catholic Studies, and the second by one of her former students, Maurice Nutt, C.Ss. R., D.Min.

I Knew Sister Thea Bowman

Cyprian Davis, O.S.B.
Saint Meinrad Archabbey

My friendship with Sister Thea Bowman began with faculty membership in the Institute for Black Catholic Studies in the summer of 1980 (1984) at Xavier University in Louisiana. Those were the "glory" days of pioneer and new initiatives. From the beginning, Sister Thea was like one whom I had never known before. It has to be admitted that I was this very "prim and proper" Benedictine monk whose preconceptions were waiting to be shattered by a remarkable Franciscan nun.

Our institute faculty was small. We came to know each other, inside and out. The Holy Spirit was alive. He made us all reconfigured with joy. Often we were on the River walk in the Quarter in the evening. Sister Thea came singing with an aria from Puccini, followed by a Gospel hymn and then a Spiritual. I was mortified. Nuns do not do that. She was overjoyed. I am sure that the angels took up the song.

Sister Thea taught me a lot about living and about dying. She also taught me about fearing and freedom. She was extraordinary. All who worked with her and taught with her came to know this in one way or another. She would never want to be called "extraordinary." But the truth is that she had a gift in making us all a little bit out of the ordinary.

Dom. Cyprian Davis, O.S.B., a Benedictine priest since 1956, is Professor of Church History at Saint Meinrad Archabbey. He also serves as archivist for Saint Meinrad Archabbey, the Swiss-American Congregation of Benedictines, for the National Black Catholic Clergy Caucus, and for the Black Catholic Theological Symposium, and is a founding member of the National Black Clergy Caucus and the BCTS, out of which arose the Institute for Black Catholic Studies.

Thea Bowman: The Courage To Keep On Keeping On!

Maurice J. Nutt, C.Ss.R.
Hampton University

In an interview for the popular news program *60 Minutes* in 1987, Sister Thea Bowman, F.S.P.A., told Mike Wallace, "I think the difference between me and some other people is that I am content to do my little bit. Sometimes people think they have to do big things in order to make change. If each one of us would light the candle, we've got a tremendous light."[1]

Remaining true to those words, Sister Thea Bowman crowded a lot of "little bit" into her fifty-two years. In retrospect, much of what she did transcended the adjective "little." She made decisions and faced situations that required a great deal of courage and influenced thousands. Part of her "little bit" philosophy was "to try." Before she died in 1990, she said she hoped her tombstone inscription would read "She tried." Her wish was later granted.

Known as Bertha during her childhood, Sister Thea was born in Yazoo City, Mississippi, in 1937 and subsequently spent most of her childhood in nearby Canton. Her physician father, Theon, cared for many of Canton's Black citizens. Her mother, Esther, was a teacher who instilled in Thea a love for learning and an appreciation of the arts and culture. She also hoped her daughter would be a proper, sophisticated, and sweet young lady. Thea, however, had a penchant to be bold, loud, and exuberant. At a very young age, she exhibited her tendency to search for meaning in life and to hold fast to what she believed. At the age of ten, this only child of Protestant parents decided to be baptized into the Catholic Church.

Both Theon and Esther realized the importance of a good education for their daughter, but the educational system for Black children in Canton was very poor. A year after Thea's baptism, her mother enrolled her in the newly opened Holy Child Jesus School,

---

[1] CBS 60 Minutes, "Interview with Thea Bowman" by news anchor Mike Wallace (May, 1987).

founded by the Franciscan Sisters of Perpetual Adoration in a salvaged army barracks. "After six years of public schooling, it was perfect joy," Thea wrote during her novitiate. "When Sister Mildred Burger became my teacher, she put me through eight levels of *Think and Do* books in one year....My friends and I were challenged every day to learn and help someone else. I was poor in math, so someone had to coach me. I was good in reading, so I had to help someone else."[2]

The welcoming, positive experience at Holy Child Jesus School contrasted with the rest of society's attitude toward people of color. Thea witnessed the disrespect, rejection, and oppression inflicted on her people. But despite the prejudice she encountered, her mother cautioned her never to retaliate. "Returning insults makes you small like they are,"[3] Esther said. Thea realized years later that she had been called to be a bridge of understanding and a peacemaker among various cultures.

Even more than the theology or doctrine of the Catholic Church, the way in which Catholics seemed to love and care for one another inspired Thea to become Catholic. The Sisters at Holy Child Jesus School, who lived a religion that was real and relevant and put their faith into action, impressed Thea, and she yearned to be part of their order. But when she announced her desire to join the Franciscan Sisters, her distraught parents refused permission until Thea went on a hunger strike. Young Bertha, described as a very agreeable person, could also be firm in her convictions. Thus, at the age of fifteen, Bertha headed north to LaCrosse, Wisconsin, taking with her many precious gifts—gifts she had learned from those she called the "old folks," or elders, in her life. She had learned their coping mechanisms and survival skills needed during generations of oppression. Thea also carried with her the richness of her African American heritage and culture—its history, stories, music, songs, dances, rituals, prayers, symbols, foods, customs, and traditions. She also carried courage in her heart; in the

---

[2] Judy Ball, "A Woman Wrapped in Courage," *Mustard Seed* (January 6, 1989): 1-2.

[3] *Sr. Thea: Her Own Story* (Video), Oblate Media and Communications, Florissant, MO. 1990.

convent, hers was to be the only Black face.

To honor her father, Bertha took "Thea," which means "of God," as her religious name. After professing her first vows, Thea began teaching at Blessed Sacrament School in LaCrosse, and then returned to Canton to teach English and music at Holy Child Jesus High School. After ten years, Thea's Franciscan superiors recognized that she would be an excellent college professor. In 1968, Thea began graduate studies in English at Catholic University in Washington, DC.

The 1960s had been a time of turbulent transformation for the nation. Racial strife, riots, the Civil Rights Act, marches on Washington and in the South, church bombings, the assassinations of Martin Luther King, Jr., President John F. Kennedy, and Robert F. Kennedy—a quest for justice and equality confronted the nation. Likewise, the late 1960s provided a time of transformation for Thea.

Far from the "old folks" in Mississippi and the solitude, sanctuary, and shelter of LaCrosse, Thea found soulful solace in the extended Black community in urban Washington. The liturgical renewal of the Second Vatican Council had encouraged her to discover her African American religious heritage and prompted her to enter her Church "fully functioning," as she described it. She embraced her Blackness; being Black was good. Expressing her ancestral customs within the rather staid Western European liturgy was good, even desirable; Thea welcomed the Vatican II documents that encouraged the integration of ethnic rituals, including dance, into the liturgy. But she needed courage to own and proclaim her Black Catholic heritage in her life and in her Church.

Thea delved deeper into the richness of the Black oral tradition as she studied language and linguistics. Her exploration fashioned and formed her in sharing the stories and songs of her people, and her presentations reflected the lively preaching heard in traditional Black churches. Though women do not preach from the pulpit in the Catholic Church, Thea proclaimed she could preach everywhere else—in school, on the train, on the street corner.

Thea truly did preach everywhere. After completing her doctorate and traveling and studying in Europe, she returned to the classroom, this time at Viterbo College (now University) in LaCrosse, where she challenged and encouraged her students to think for themselves. Thea strongly believed that the students' opinions were as valid as hers as long as they could support their opinions with evidence. She taught by example as powerfully as by word.

Thea's entrance into higher education provided her with an even broader arena for "preaching." She became a popular speaker on the college circuit, sharing her gift of Blackness in vibrant presentations that always included song. Thea challenged others to look beyond themselves, to look respectfully at others. She emphasized that cultural awareness required a spirit of mutuality: She was willing to learn about other cultures, and she asked others to walk with and appreciate with her the glory of Black culture.

As Thea's reputation spread, her parents aged, and in 1978 she returned to Mississippi to care for them. Her bishop in Jackson, Mississippi, asked her to serve as a consultant to the Diocesan Office of Intercultural Awareness; she eventually served as director, expanding her efforts to assail racial prejudice and promote cultural awareness and sensitivity. She became even more passionate in her vocation to speak and write about the significance of Black spirituality, history, culture, and song, about the Black family, and especially about being Black and Catholic.

Two years later, Thea helped found the Institute for Black Catholic Studies (IBCS) at Xavier University in New Orleans and served on the faculty. Once again, she brought her indomitable spirit, engaging personality, and prophetic vision to the Institute's mission to provide an intellectual, spiritual, pastoral, and cultural immersion into the Black Catholic experience. Thea taught courses in Black literature, Black preaching, Black spirituals and songs and art. Thea's classes were more than scholarly lectures; they were life-changing encounters.

As an educator, Thea's pedagogy was to motivate her students to be self-determined and inquisitive learners. On more than one occasion while teaching at the Institute for Black Catholic Studies she would abruptly stop the class lecture to make sure that her students were not merely memorizing the subject material but fully comprehending and internalizing the lesson. She would often quip, "So what does this [subject matter] have to do with your life, your family, your community or your lived-experience?"

Humorously she would challenge her students by asking the ambiguous yet loaded question: "Who's teaching this class?" If her students responded, "you're teaching this class," she would then ask "are you sure? Am I teaching this class or are you teachers as well?" The point she was impressing upon her students was that in the educational process through dialogue, examination and exploration we learn from one another. She wanted her "disciples" to be confident in the learning environment that they were both learners and teachers. "Each one teach one" was her constant mantra.

Thea would often ask her students to self-evaluate; to give themselves a grade. Thea would look intently at the grades the students had given themselves and ask the students why they gave themselves that particular grade. If the students either overrated or underrated themselves, Thea would gently tell the students to "think long and hard" and re-evaluate themselves. There were times when students would continue to under-rate themselves and she would let the grade stand! This experimentation was a lesson in itself for her students to be both truthful and confident in their abilities.

In 1984, Thea faced the biggest challenge of her life. Both of her parents died, and she was diagnosed with breast cancer vowing to "live until I die," Thea courageously continued her rigorous schedule of speaking engagements. As the cancer spread to her bones, she did not stop being a courageous witness for the Lord. Bald from the effects of chemotherapy and dressed in her customary colorful African garb, Thea arrived at her presentations in a wheelchair.

Despite unrelenting pain and her deteriorating condition, Thea accepted an unprecedented invitation—to speak to the U.S. bishops at their annual June meeting in 1989 at Seton Hall University. Thea spoke of the Church as her "home," her "family of families," and described her effort to find her way to that home. She instructed and enlightened the bishops on Black history and spirituality. She challenged them to continue to evangelize the Black community, to promote inclusivity and full participation of Blacks within Church leadership, and to understand the necessity and value of Catholic schools within the Black community. She told them the "true truth" of what it meant to be Black in America—and to be a Black Catholic.

Then, in her soft Southern drawl, this petite, frail woman with big bright eyes and a pleasant smile invited the bishops to cross their arms, join hands, and move together as they sang "We Shall Overcome." Tears and thunderous applause followed.

Thea knew no stranger. She offered compassion to the young man living with AIDS. She enjoyed a hearty laugh with her beloved "old folks." She met and enchanted celebrities such as Harry Belafonte and Whoopi Goldberg. She encouraged single mothers. She spoke strong words couched in love to the Roman Catholic hierarchy. Yet her greatest testimony may have been the way she faced death, living until the end. That inspirational courage, that outlook, speaks to all cultures.

During her fifty-two years on Earth, Thea Bowman wove the diverse elements of her life into a garment as vivid and lively as her African garb. She was simultaneously an "old folks" child, a devoted Franciscan, an advocate of all cultures while maintaining her love for her "own Black self," a proud maiden of Mississippi, a persuasive preacher, a tenacious teacher, a soul-stirring singer, a lover of the Church, a teller of the "true truth," a faithful friend, a spiritual mother to many, and an instrument of peace, love, and joy. Before she died, she declared, "I want people to remember that I tried to love the Lord...that I tried to love, and how that computes is immaterial."[4]   She tried to weave that garment until the very end—little bit by little bit.

At five o'clock on the morning of March 30, 1990, Thea was attended by her dear friend and fellow Franciscan Sister Dorothy Kundinger, F.S.P.A., who had traveled with and helped care for her. Sister Dorothy reports that Thea was sitting almost upright to improve her breathing. "I said, 'Thea, many friends have said goodbye. It's OK to die....Your Mama and your Daddy...are waiting for you in heaven. Don't be afraid. You're not alone. I love you. Goodbye, Thea.' Thea's head turned to the side and her shoulders dropped. She didn't try to open her eyes anymore."[5]

Sister Thea Bowman has been called a saint, and many are working to have her recognized as such by the Church. But according to Sister Francesca Thompson, OSF, Thea "has already been canonized in the hearts and souls of those who knew and loved her." Let the Church say "Amen!"

Maurice J. Nutt, C.Ss.R., D.Min., a Redemptorist priest for 21 years, holds a doctor of ministry in preaching from Aquinas Institute of Theology in St. Louis, Missouri. He teaches in the Religious Studies Distance Learning Program at Hampton University in Hampton, Virginia, and is a faculty member at the Institute for Black Catholic Studies (IBCS) at Xavier University in New Orleans, Louisiana. Father Nutt serves as pastor of Holy Names of Jesus and Mary Catholic Church in Memphis, Tennessee.

---

[4] Sister Thea Bowman, *Almost Home, Living With Suffering and Dying*, (DVD), Liguori Publications, Liguori, MO. 2008.
[5] Sister Dorothy Kundinger, F.S.P.A., from her personal journal, April, 1990.

Thirty Years and Counting! The Institute for Black Catholic Studies – 1980-2010

The Institute for Black Catholic Studies arose out of a passion for authentically Black and truly Catholic theology and ministry in 1980. It continues to inspire its students, its faculty, and all those who are touched by its unique approach and identity. Kathleen Dorsey Bellow and C. Vanessa White reflect on the history and mission of the IBCS.

A Thirty Year Collaboration in Uniquely Black and Catholic Mission

Kathleen Dorsey Bellow
Xavier University of New Orleans, Louisiana

Xavier University of Louisiana (XULA) is a relatively small institution with a sizeable reputation. The XULA website publicizes many of its claims to fame. Established in 1925 by St. Katharine Drexel and the Sisters of the Blessed Sacrament, Xavier is the only historically Black and Catholic university in the United States. From this unique identity flows the stated mission of the school to "contribute to the promotion of a more just and humane society by preparing its students to assume roles of leadership and service in a global society."[1]

Its president, Dr. Norman C. Francis (Class of '52) has the longest-running tenure of any president of an American university. When U.S. President Barack Obama visited New Orleans last month to mark the 5-year anniversary of Hurricane Katrina that devastated coastal Mississippi and Louisiana, he spoke from Xavier University, partly in tribute to the determined leadership of President Francis who spearheaded the school's amazing rebound in the aftermath of the storm.

---

[1] "Catholic Mission and Ministry". Xavier University of Louisiana.
< http://www.xula.edu/catholic/index.php> (Accessed 6 September 2011).

Xavier continues to recover. Fall 2010 student enrollment is at a new post-Katrina high. New construction projects dot the campus and a long-awaited chapel is on the drawing board. Amid the distractions of recovery and new growth, the university has maintained its standard of preparing students for life. From the XULA website:

> According to the U.S. Department of Education, Xavier continues to rank first nationally in the number of African American students earning undergraduate degrees in biology, chemistry and physics.
>
> The College of Pharmacy, one of only two pharmacy schools in Louisiana, is among the nation's top three producers of African American Doctor of Pharmacy degree recipients.
>
> Xavier ranks first in the nation in placing African American students into medical schools and has held that rank since 1993.[2]

Through these aspects of vocation and life at Xavier, one can see faith actively expressed in Christian discipleship.

Faith sustains another less heralded work in progress at Xavier University. The Institute for Black Catholic Studies took up residence at Xavier University thirty years ago as a graduate theology program to cultivate scholarship that is Black and Catholic. The project grew out of an idea proposed by Fr. August Taylor to the National Black Catholic Clergy Caucus (NBCCC) in 1969 that was tested in the first Black Catholic Theological Symposium that convened in 1978 at the Motherhouse of the Oblate Sisters of Providence in Baltimore. In 1979, a committee of African American women and men religious drafted a plan that was refined in numerous consultations. Jamie T. Phelps, O.P. was a key consultant. Thaddeus Posey, O.F.M., Cap. shaped a final

---

[2] "Quick Facts University and Media Relations." Xavier University of Louisiana. 28 May 2010. http://www.xula.edu/mediarelations/quickfacts.php (6 September 2011).

proposal that he presented to the NBCCC. With NBCCC support, Fr. Posey and Dr. Norman Francis championed the cause with the Xavier administration and the local bishops. In 1980, the Institute for Black Catholic Studies became a resident graduate theology program on the Xavier University campus that has met every summer since (except 2006, in the aftermath of Hurricane Katrina when the Institute was hosted at the University of Notre Dame).

The IBCS was born out of the community's contention that U.S. Black Catholics have a right and responsibility to participate in humanity's ongoing dialogue about who God is and how we are to live as God's children. Over the years this discussion has broadened the church's self-understanding by adding African and African American dimension to the study and practice of the Catholic faith. The disciplines of church history, ethics, theology, scripture, aesthetics, liturgy, spirituality and catechetics have been enriched by the Institute's rigorous academic tradition that immerses students and faculty in the Black Catholic cultures of New Orleans and Xavier.

The mission of the IBCS is to form lay persons, religious and clergy for more effective ministry in the Black community and in the church at-large. The IBCS message is the gospel of Christ proclaimed through Black life. Responding to the critical needs and building on the indomitable strengths of its constituent communities, the structure of the Institute is unapologetically intense. In the Masters of Theology, Certificate and Enrichment programs members learn and teach Catholic Christian discipleship in classroom and out, working grace-fully through the challenges and joys of community life. From Morning Prayer through daily classes to evening African drumming and dance enrichments, the community grows together in a healthy sense of Godliness - intellectually, spiritually, culturally and socially. The benefits flow out from the IBCS and Xavier University of Louisiana to community and Church.

In these thirty years, the Institute for Black Catholic Studies of Xavier University has produced some 68 Masters of Theology graduates, at least nine of whom have earned doctoral degrees in theology or related fields. A total roster of Certificate and Enrichment program attendees has yet to be tallied, but what is remarkable is that a number who began or advanced their church studies in the summer in New Orleans have continued theological pursuits.

Unlike the sciences, it is difficult to quantify Xavier University of Louisiana's theological contributions to the Church. Given the student accomplishment of both its undergraduate Theology Department and the Institute for Black Catholic Studies, Xavier University is serious about Catholic mission.

Following through in its departmental mission to form more effective, healthy and culturally- competent ministers, the IBCS has potential to stretch Xavier University, the Black Catholic community and the Church at-large to more intentionally use the gifts of Black culture in teaching and evangelizing God's people. Lessons in Christian community learned during the IBCS summer are useful for challenging and inspiring us all year-long and all life-long.

At this 30 year juncture, let us celebrate the enduring faithfulness of Xavier University and the evolving vocation of the Institute for Black Catholic Studies. Thank God, our ancestors in faith, and steadfast leadership for a holy collaboration that "contribute(s) to the promotion of a more just and humane society by preparing its students to assume roles of leadership and service in a global society."[3]

Kathleen Dorsey Bellow, ThM, D.Min., currently serves as principal of Sacred Heart St. Katharine Drexel Catholic School in Lake Charles and Associate Director for Certificate and Enrichment Programs, Institute for Black Catholic Studies of Xavier University of Louisiana.

---

[3]"Catholic Mission and Ministry". Xavier University of Louisiana. < http://www.xula.edu/catholic/index.php> (Accessed 6 September 2011).

Thirty Years of Impact: The Institute for Black Catholic Studies

C. Vanessa White
Catholic Theological Union

This year marks the thirtieth anniversary of the Institute for Black Catholic Studies at Xavier University of Louisiana (1980-2010). As it states in its program literature, the Institute offers a holistic graduate theology program and certificate and enrichment programs that form students academically, theologically, socially, and spiritually for effective Catholic ministry in the Black community and in the Church at large. As Dr. Kathleen Dorsey Bellow has noted, the Institute has graduated 68 men and women with master's degrees in theology and countless more men and women have participated in its continuing education programs.

While in New Orleans in 1987, Pope John Paul II encouraged Black Catholics to share their gifts of Blackness. He specifically called on Black Catholics "to give priority to the great task of evangelization, to be missionaries of Christ's love and truth with your own black community."[1] Black Catholics have taken up this mission the ongoing presence, work and impact of the Institute for Black Catholics Studies.

Thus far ten graduates of the master's of theology program of the Institute for Black Catholic Studies have continued their formal theological education and have received doctorates in theology or ministry.[2] Many graduates and alumni of the Institute

---

[1] Pope John Paul II in "The Papal Visit," 17 September 1987, *New York Times* online. http://www.nytimes.com/1987/09/13/us/the-papal-visit-address-to-the-pope-by-a-black-bishop-and-john-paul-s-reply.html?pagewanted+2 (Accessed 12 September 2010).

[2] The Ph.D. graduates include Sister Addie Lorraine Walker, SSND, Father Roy Lee, LaReine-Marie Mosely, and Father Donald Chambers. Graduates having earned the Doctorate in Ministry include Kathleen Dorsey Bellow, Sister Eva Lumas, SSS, Sr. Eva Regina Martin, S.S.F., Father Maurice Nutt, C.SS.R., Father Freddy Washington, C.S.Sp., and Sister Oralisa Martin.

are now professors at seminaries and colleges throughout the United States.[3] They have also contributed to ongoing theological conversations by publishing books and articles in respected journals and by serving on a variety of editorial boards.[4] Institute scholars have presented papers at theological and historical society meetings around the country.[5]

The Institute was the birthplace for programs that have had a tremendous impact on the Black Catholic community. The Archbishop James Patterson Lyke Conference had its beginnings in the graduate research done by Fr. Ferdinand Cheri, O.F.M. on liturgy and music at the Institute for Black Catholic Studies. Similarly, Sr. Dr. Oralisa Martin developed the ORACLE Summer

---

[3] Dr. LaReine-Marie Mosely teaches at Loyola University in Chicago, Sr. Dr. Eva Marie Lumas, SSS teaches at the Franciscan School of Theology in Berkley, Fr. Dr. Maurice Nutt, CSSR teaches for Hampton University in Virginia, Dr. C. Vanessa White teaches at the Catholic Theological Union in Chicago, Fr. Dr. Roy Lee teaches for St. Leo University in Atlanta, Georgia, Fr. Derran Combs, OFM teaches at the University of St. Francis in Joliet, Illinois, and Sr. Dr. Shawnee Daniels Sykes, SSND teaches at Mt. Mary College in Milwaukee, Wisconsin. Several graduates and alumni have also returned to teach at the Institute for Black Catholic Studies in the master's degree program and in the certificate and enrichment programs.

[4] Cecilia A. Moore and Eva Lumas, SSS (*U.S. Catholic Historian*), Shawnee Daniels Sykes, SSND, Eva Lumas, SSS, C. Vanessa White, Maurice Nutt, CSSR (*New Theology Review*), Shawnee Daniels Sykes, SSND (*Health Progress*). Graduates and alumni also serve on publication editorial boards. Shawnee Daniels Sykes, SSND serves on the Institute for Catholic Bioethics at St. Joseph's University in Philadelphia and C. Vanessa White serves on the *New Theology Review*. LaReine-Marie Mosely co-edited *Uncommon Faithfulness: The Black Catholic Experience* with M. Shawn Copeland and Albert J. Raboteau, Maurice Nutt, CSSR edited *Sr. Thea: In Her Own Words*, C. Vanessa White, Cecilia A. Moore and Paul M. Marshall, S.M. co-edited *Songs of Our Hearts and Meditations of Our Souls: Prayers for Black Catholics,* and Father Ferdinand Cheri, O.F.M. and Marcia A. Berry contributed to the forthcoming *New African American Catholic Hymnal* to be published by GIA.

[5] Examples of such presentations include: LaReine-Marie Mosely, Shawnee Daniels Sykes, SSND, C. Vanessa White (Catholic Theological Society of America), LaReine-Marie Mosely (Society for the Study of Black Religion), Kathleen Dorsey Bellow, Shawnee Daniels Sykes, SSN, C. Vanessa White, Fr. Roy Lee (Black Catholic Theological Symposium) and Orita B. Edwards (Seventh Triennial Conference on the History of Women Religious at the University of Notre Dame).

Institute for Youth. Sr. Thea Bowman's influence can be seen in the workshops, seminars, and courses offered by many Institute graduates, but most notably in those offered by Fr. Dr. Maurice Nutt, CSSR in preaching.

In 1980, when the Institute for Black Catholic Studies began, there were few African American lay ministerial leaders in decision making roles in dioceses throughout the nation. Today Institute graduates, current students, and alumni are directors of religious education, pastoral associates, principals and teachers in Catholic schools, directors of pastoral offices, retreat and conference facilitators, workshop presenters, spiritual directors, and social justice ministers. Most recently members of the Institute for Black Catholic Studies faculty have been invited to participate in the 2011 National Symposium on Lay Ecclesial Ministry.[6]

In the thirty years since its formation, the Institute for Black Catholic Studies continues to break ground as the only program of its kind that teaches from a distinctly Black Catholic perspective. Its impact is seen in the lives and ministries of its students, faculty, and staff. It is with profound gratitude that we acknowledge the vision and sacrifices of the early founders of the Institute, Fr. Augustus Taylor, Fr. Dr. Thaddeus Posey, O.F.M., Cap., Fr. David Benz, Dr. Toinette Eugene, Fr. Dr. Joseph Nearon, SSS, Bishop Terry Steib, S.V.D., Sr. Dr. Francesca Thompson, O.S.F. and Sr. Dr. Jamie T. Phelps, O.P. As the Institute for Black Catholic Studies enters its thirty-first year, may its members continue to be open to the Holy Spirit.

Dr. C. Vanessa White is Assistant Professor of Spirituality and the Director of the Augustus Tolton Pastoral Ministry Program at Catholic Theological Union in Chicago. She is also the Coordinator of Spiritual Formation and a member of the Master's Degree faculty and Certificate and Enrichment Program faculty at Xavier University of Louisiana's Institute for Black Catholic Studies.

---

[6] C. Vanessa White and timone davis.

Cyprian Davis's Contributions to the Study of African American Catholic History: Articles in the *U.S. Catholic Historian*

Christopher J. Kauffman
Editor of *U.S. Catholic Historian*

In celebration of Father Cyprian Davis's eightieth birthday, the BCTS invited his friend and fellow historian, Dr. Christopher Kauffman to reflect on the meaning of Father Cyprian's articles published in the U.S. Catholic Historian from 1986 to 2006. Dr. Kauffman pays special attention to the relationship of these articles to Father Cyprian's 1990 study The History of Black Catholics in the United States, to his inspirational writings, and to his ongoing research and writing of Black Catholic history.

In the pages of our *USCH* Winter 2010 issue, seven historians honored Father Cyprian Davis. Now I have the pleasure of contributing an article on Cyprian's work in the *Journal of the Black Catholic Theological Symposium*. I pleasantly recall many dinners we have shared during the evenings of academic conferences. At one meeting he gave me a copy of the first issue of the *Symposium*. He grinned with pride knowing I was unaware of its first publication.

As editor of the *USCH* I am grateful to have published six articles of his over a period of twenty years, from 1986 to 2006. Cyprian's gifts to our journal have underscored our niche as a publication committed to vital themes and greatly contributed to the advancement of fine history. This article will explore three themes: the making of his 1990 book *The History of Black Catholics in the United States*, his inspirational articles and a few glimpses into the soon to be revised edition of his book.

Father Cyprian's first articles for us, "Black Catholics in Nineteenth Century America" anchored the issue titled "The Black Catholic Experience". Focusing on the 19th century this piece reveals some realities which were significantly expanded within his classic book. The first trend was the Catholic Church's complicity with slavery: priests, bishops, religious communities of women and men owning slaves while only European Catholic leaders opposed slavery. The second is "Elements of Sanctity": the foundation of the Oblate Sisters of Providence by Elizabeth Lange, assisted by Father James Hector Joubert, S.S., and the Sisters of the Holy Family founded by Juliette Gaudin and Henriette Delille. Father Cyprian tells the story of three black priests, the sons of Michael Morris Healy, a farmer in Georgia and Eliza their slave mother. This couple sent their sons to be educated in the North. Three of them were ordained in European seminaries and held prominent positions in the church in the U.S. Patrick Francis, who passed for white, became President of Georgetown University; Sherwood Alexander was appointed chancellor of the Diocese of Boston and James Augustine was appointed Bishop of Portland, Maine. None of the Healy brothers identified with the Black Catholic community. Cyprian concludes his article with the story of Daniel Rudd, a former slave who in 1886 founded the *American Catholic Tribune*, a Black Catholic weekly newspaper and who, three years later, initiated the first Black Catholic Congress held at St. Augustine's black parish in Washington, D.C. Father Augustus Tolton the first black priests in the U.S. recited a Solemn High Mass and Cardinal James Gibbons preached on the opening day of the Congress. The delegates went on record calling for Catholic schools, the opening of labor unions to blacks, improved housing and other social programs. There were four more Congresses, attended by lawyers, doctors, librarians, state legislators and others who expressed "to a national audience their sense of identity, their pride and their sense of confidence as Catholics and as Blacks." Though the delegates consistently asserted their deep loyalty to the Church the agendas of these subsequent congresses became more demanding, with an almost military tone. Without thorough documentary evidence Cyprian considered this latter attitude the rationale for the bishops' calling for the termination of the Black Congress movement after its fifth meeting.

This issue of the *USCH* so expanded the historical self-understanding of the Black Catholic community that there was a demand to publish more copies. Because we underestimated the extent of market demand, particularly among diocesan offices of Black Catholic Ministry, we published a third edition. The three editions also, of course, enhanced our journal's general readership.

Father Cyprian's second article was in the Historical Analysis section of a double issue titled "The Catholic Community 1800-1987." The front six articles were followed by a second section of two reflections on the National Office of Black Catholics and a brief piece on Offices of Black Catholic Ministry. The final section featured nine brief theological, sociological and historical papers which had been presented at the "sixth" National Black Catholic Congress held finally at The Catholic University of America on May 21-24, 1987. I was present at the event to underscore our intention to publish the proceedings of that Congress. We staffed a *USCH* table to extend our gratitude for the great interest in "The Black Catholic Experience," to provide copies at a good price and to add new subscribers among the hundred in attendance.

Cyprian's article was "The Holy See and American Black Catholics: a Forgotten Chapter in American Catholic History." While his first article regarding the five Black Catholic Congresses totaled only three pages, this next article devoted twelve pages to the movement, symbolic of a vast amount of new research. The last nine pages indicate the impressive extent of Cyprian's research in the Archives of Propaganda Fide in Rome and in the so-called Secret Archives of the Vatican. In the Archives of Propaganda Fide he found a January 1904 letter from Cardinal Girolamo Maria Gotti, Prefect of the Congregation of Propaganda Fide to Archbishop Diomede Falconio, the Apostolic Delegate to the US, about reports "that in some of the dioceses of the United States the conditions of the Catholic negroes, not only in respect to their faithful but also in respect to their pastor and bishops is very humiliating and entirely different from that of the whites." Gotti asked Falconio to call this to the attention of Cardinal James Gibbons so that a gradual improvement of conditions could transpire and lead to a removal of these inequalities. There was no evidence of Gibbons having initiated any inquiry about these humiliating conditions.

Later, from 1912 to 1921, two curial cardinals wrote letters to the apostolic delegate. They noted three principal concerns. They wanted to adopt a plan for evangelizing Black Catholics and to create an effective contingent of missionaries prepared to pool their resources to engage the apostolate to the Afro-American community. Father Cyprian said "Here the supposition was [that] a nation-wide ordinariate or independent episcopal jurisdiction for Black Catholics in America would probably be the most effective [means]." The third concern was for ending discrimination against Blacks through Catholic instructions of high learning, especially Catholic University, and the ordination of Black men to the priesthood. The bishops generally opposed the ordinariate. The Cardinal agreed to a provisional delay of the ordinariate and was satisfied to know there was an indication of preparing men for ordination. Though I am merely highlighting a portion of this article, Cyprian's fine book fully narrates the Roman concerns and elaborates on other topics in a long chapter.

Inspirational Articles

Our double issue Winter/Spring 1989 was Spirituality, Devotionalism and Popular Religion. Three of the ten articles were related to Black Catholics: "Down at the Cross: Afro-American Spirituality" by Albert Raboteau; "A Contemporary Pilgrimage: Personal Testimony of Blessed Katherine Drexel's Spirituality" by Roland Lagarde, S.B.S.; and "Black Spirituality" by Cyprian Davis.

Cyprian opens his article with a narrative of the Holy Family Society whose purpose was to provide the "colored people an opportunity of attending more particularly to their salvation and spiritual concerns." This quote comes from Father John F. Hickey, the assistant priest at the Cathedral of Baltimore who kept a journal of the Holy Family Society's meetings. They met every Sunday in the basement of Calvert Hall School across from the Cathedral for twenty-two months, December of 1843 to October of 1845. The society, numbering between 150 to 250 people, recited traditional prayers and sang English hymns. Cyprian reported that "There was at times spontaneous prayer."

The core of the article, however, is an elaboration of what the black bishops stated in their pastoral letter titled *What We Have Seen and Heard*. "Black spirituality has four major characteristics: It is contemplative. It is holistic. It is joyful. It is communitarian." To quote further from this piece would detract from its inspirational character. He refers to spirituals, to African roots, to the emotional and joyful prayers of the Holy Family Society, and to many examples of the devotion to Black saints, "the saints of dark and beautiful skins and dancing eyes."

Our Winter 1994 issue titled, "African Americans and Their Church," was intended to generate new research among graduate students and seasoned historians. Cyprian urged study beyond the African identity of the early 19th century to further and deeper meanings of 'Black American Catholic thought." He also urged research to develop prosopographical studies. Research in archives of women religious who served Black parishes could yield valuable material on parish devotional life. He wished to see more attention given beyond the extensive publications about priests, bishops and religious as slave owners and to focus on Catholic abolitionists, including those in Europe who deserve further study. Among African American artists warranting research he mentioned "Mary Lou Williams, convert, Jazz pianist, composer of religious music."

Our spring of 2004 issue titled, "African American Spirituality and Liturgical Renewal," advanced this notion of future studies. The Contents Cover reads:

> "African American Spirituality: Scenes, Stories and Meanings" by Cyprian L. Rowe; "Some Reflections on African American Spirituality" by Cyprian Davis, O.S.B., "We Come This Far by Faith: Black Catholics and Their Church" by Diana L. Hayes; "The Emergence of African American Catholic Worship" by Mary E. McGann and Eva Marie Lumas; *The African American Hymnal* and the African American Spiritual" by M. Shawn Copeland; "This is My Story, This My Song: The Historiography of Vatican II, Black Catholic Identity, Jazz and the Religious Compositions of Mary Lou Williams" by Tammy Lynn Kernodle; "Freeing the Spirit: Very Personal Reflections on One Man's Search for Spirit in Worship" by Clarence Rufus J. Rivers.

Cyprian's article on African American Spirituality opens and closes with a focus on Daniel Rudd's columns in the *American Catholic Tribune*. He refers to Rudd's sense of 'mission': Black Catholics should be the "leaven which would raise up their people not only before God but before men... like yeast...that makes the whole batch of dough leavened," and "The number of Black Catholics might be small, but, like the Kingdom, they can transform the entire Black American community." He also cites the work of Nwaka Egbulem, a noted Nigerian theologian who captures African spirituality and summarizes: "All things find their origin in God and His Presence permeates all things. The individual is incomplete without the extended family and the community. There is power in the oral tradition; there is power in the environment in which we live."

In a lengthy narrative Cyprian notes the influence of the African values of the Nguzo Saba had upon African American Catholics and presents English translations of the Swahili names as unity, self-determination, collective work, cooperative economics, creativity and faith. After an exploration of the Seven

Virtues he returns to cite again Daniel Rudd's "call to be leaven among Black Americans." In spite of slavery and years of excessive racial discriminations Black Catholics "helped build a church; as parishioners they were forced to the back of the same churches. Still as Catholics they sang their own songs prayed in their own cadences and practiced their own virtues. They found their own spaces in a sometimes hostile bra of Catholicism, into which their own spirit was with God's grace and thereby enriched the spirituality of the Catholic Church today."

In the fall 2006 issue titled, "Catholics in the South," Cyprian Davis contributed the article "Black Catholics in the Civil Rights Movement in the Southern United States: A.P. Tureaud, Thomas Wyatt Turner and Earl Johnson." His 1990 book included an analysis of Turner and he takes on a new perspective within this comparative study. Readers of the revised book will be impressed with Tureaud (1899-1972) who was a native of New Orleans and a graduate of Howard University Law School. Between 1937 and 1947...he was the only Black lawyer practicing in Louisiana. Three of his cases involved removing inequalities between salaries of white and black public school teachers. After the 1954 Supreme Court decision to mandate desegregation of schools he worked to implement the decision and confronted excessive and bitter opponents who used delay among other tactics with the intention of maintaining segregation. Tureaud was so committed to the court system and to the "sanctity of the law, he did not agree to public demonstrations to promote change. However, when demonstrators were arrested he took on their cases to protect their rights. Cyprian concludes: "Quiet and unassuming he would become one of the most influential Catholics of the twentieth century Catholic Church today."

Cyprian's article on Thomas Wyatt Turner (1877-1978) reveals his admiration of him. He received his Ph.D. in Biology yet it was in his role as leader of the Committee for the Advancement of Colored Catholics and later of the Federated Colored Catholics that Turner achieved national recognition as the dominant voice against discrimination in Church and society. His early agenda included ordaining black priests and he organized the Federated Colored Catholics to struggle against racial discrimination in the Church. The organization grew to 100,000 members by 1932. Two white Jesuit priests considered it a throwback to the Jim Crow Separatist era and they formed the Catholic Interracial Conference of New York; without vital new leadership the Federated disbanded in 1952. Cyprian concludes: "By this time the Civil Rights Movement had moved in a new direction with new leadership. Ironically, Turner's ideal of direct action, self-motivation and non-clerical responsibility became the order of the day. Turner was ahead of his time. Had his proposals prevailed, there would have become a greater horizon and a richer racial understanding."

Earl Johnson (1928-1988), a graduate of Howard University's Law School in 1958, became what Cyprian termed a bridge builder. Settling in his wife's hometown of Jacksonville, Florida he became president of the NAACP. He soon committed his practice to desegregating the schools of the Duval County school system; eleven years later they become fully integrated. Johnson, the first Black member of the Jacksonville Bar Association, defended young Black demonstrators engaging in sit-ins. When Klansmen and members of the White Citizen Councils attacked Blacks led by some young members of the NAACP riots ensued and only when met with armed resistance did the police bring an end to the violence. Johnson was recognized as a local hero and honest broker in the 1960 and 1964 riots. His leadership led to elections to political office; Cyprian calls Johnson, like Thomas More, "a man for all seasons."

Thank you, dear Cyprian, for the many gifts you've given to the readers of the *USCH* and for your friendship over the years.

Since 1982, Dr. Christopher Kauffman has edited the U.S. Catholic Historian. He is retired from the School of Theology and Religious Studies of the Catholic University of America where he held the Catholic Daughters of the Americas Chair in American Catholic History.

Cyprian Davis, O.S.B.
To Walk a Path, To Be Transformed, And To Transform

Cecilia Moore
University of Dayton

Kimberly Flint-Hamilton
Stetson University

This essay is Part One in a BCTS archival project to record, preserve, and publish the life stories of the senior members of our organization.

> *Do not be conformed to this world, but be transformed by the renewal of your mind, that by testing you may discern what is the will of God, what is good and acceptable and perfect. (Romans 12:2)*

On a warm summer morning we, Cecilia Moore, Kimberly Flint-Hamilton, and Steven Hamilton, sat down with Dom. Cyprian Davis, O.S.B. in his office at St. Meinrad Archabbey.[1] Classes were not yet in session so the halls were quiet. The window was open to the intermittent breeze, the gentle rain, birdsong, and the occasional roar of a lawn tractor. Cyprian's welcoming manner, with his shy, boyish smile and easy laugh,

---

[1] Cyprian Davis, O.S.B., interview by Kimberly Flint-Hamilton, Cecilia Moore, and Steven Hamilton, 5 August 2010, St. Meinrad Archabbey, Saint Meinrad, Indiana. On August 6, 2010, Father Cyprian welcomed us to the archives of the Archabbey where we got to see his profession charter and photographs chronicling his life as a Benedictine monk. This article is based on some of the important things we learned about Father Cyprian's life, work, and vocation of the course these two days of interviewing, visiting, and praying with him and the rest of the monks at Saint Meinrad. Ruth Eng's wonderful book, *Conversations in the Abbey* (St Meinrad, IN: St. Meinrad Archabbey Press, 2008) was also a valuable resource for the writing of this article.

seemed in some ways to contrast with his position as BCTS elder and patriarch. And yet in another way, his gentleness and modesty exemplify what we stand for as a scholarly community – the commitment to the fundamental humanity of all persons – and are the manifestation of a life lived according to the Rule of St. Benedict, with grace, humility, and obedience.

Numerous awards for Cyprian's contributions to various disciplines and honorary degrees lay on bookshelves or hung on the walls, testament to the profound influence he has had on Black Catholic scholarship. Also on the walls were paintings, sculpture, and other memorabilia from his trips to Africa. Cecilia and Kimberly walked around Cyprian's office looking at these as Steve performed sound checks and set up microphones. After Steve finished setting up the sound and video recording equipment, Cecilia began asking questions and Kimberly kept track of the video and interjected the occasional comment or query, while Steve mixed and balanced the audio. Laughter permeated our discussion as Cyprian reflected on his life and recalled his youth, his education, and his profound commitment to God, to Christ, and to his community at St. Meinrad.

Cyprian's life began in Washington, D.C. when he was born to Clarence W. Davis, Sr. and Evelyn Jackson Davis, on September 9, 1930 (figure 1). He was named after his father, Clarence William Davis, Jr. A few years later his sister, Evelyn, was born completing the Davis household. Clarence and his sister grew up in the Howard University neighborhood where his father taught physical education at Howard University and later at the University of the District of Columbia and his mother also taught physical education in elementary schools in the District. They grew up in a richly intellectual home and community where debate about all things was encouraged, including religion.

Figure 1: Mr. and Mrs. Davis (from the personal collection of Cyprian Davis O.S.B.)

"I was enthralled! I was in heaven!" – Fr. Cyprian Davis, O.S.B.

From the time he began reading medieval history, Clarence felt a strong attraction to the Roman Catholic Church. He loved its antiquity among other things. He wanted to know what church was like, especially the Mass. But his family was not Catholic and his parents were not particularly church-going. Though his mother was baptized a Catholic as an infant, her father had a falling-out with the parish priest when she was a small child. Her family left the Catholic Church and joined a prominent and upwardly mobile Presbyterian congregation in Washington, D.C. Clarence's parents sent him to Sunday school at the Presbyterian Church but the family did not attend Sunday church services. His parents were fairly chagrinned by Clarence's campaign to go to Mass but, being open-minded and liberal parents, they finally relented. Mrs. Davis arranged for her older brother, who had remained a Catholic, to take Clarence to Mass when he was 12 or 13. Said Cyprian, "I knew then it had to be wonderful!" And, there Clarence fell in love.

Cyprian recalled his excitement over his first-ever Catholic Mass. "I was enthralled! I was in heaven!" From then on he continued to attend Mass even though he was not yet Catholic and he determined that he would become a priest. Over the next few years he befriended several Catholics, one of whom was a monk at the English Benedictine Abbey, St. Anselm. He encouraged Clarence to contact various religious orders and request information, cautioning him also to reveal that he was a Negro in his letters since many monasteries were not open to blacks. One response encouraged Clarence to consider joining the Josephites,[2] an order dedicated to ministry in the black community. The respondent made it clear to Clarence that the order was not open to a black priest but this response did not kill Clarence's determination to become one. What this information-seeking phase did make clear to Clarence was that he needed to actually become a Catholic. Conversion to Catholicism was the next campaign he launched at home with his parents. He was not of the age yet where he could convert without parental consent. By this time, Clarence knew he wished to join a monastic order where he could both be a priest and a teacher. Becoming a Catholic was crucial to both of these things happening. So began Clarence's quest for conversion and ultimately the monastic life.

"If you are going to be a priest, be one like Thomas Verner Moore." – Clarence W. Davis, Sr.

The path to conversion and priesthood was not easy for Clarence as a black teenager. His greatest challenge came from his father, who while respectful of people of faith, was not a religious man. Mr. Davis was a black intellectual. He enjoyed the life of the mind, debate, and questioning and wanted his children to do the same. It was difficult for Mr. Davis to imagine that opportunities that he worked so hard for might not be available to his son. But young Clarence was convinced that his conversion to Catholicism and priesthood and the monastic life was not going to cut off his intellectual development. Rather, it would allow him to

---

[2] See Stephen J. Ochs, *Desegregating the Altar: The Josephites and the Struggle for Black Priests, 1871-1960* (Baton Rouge, Louisiana: Louisiana State University Press, 1993).

flourish. He argued these points with his father. Mr. Davis had studied with the renowned Catholic psychologist, Fr. Dr. Thomas Verner Moore, O.S.B., at the Catholic University of America. Mr. Davis found Father Moore to be a great thinker and an excellent teacher as well as a man of faith. Ready to accept that Clarence was going to follow this path to Catholicism and priesthood, Mr. Davis relented, saying "If you are going to be a priest, be one like Thomas Verner Moore." Although Clarence would not follow Father Moore in the field of psychology, he did join him as a Benedictine, dedicated to a life of prayer and work. With his father's acceptance, Clarence cleared the first major hurdle on his journey and at age 15, Clarence was baptized in the Roman Catholic Church.

A true lover of the Mass and prayer, young Clarence learned that the Benedictines at St. Meinrad excelled at liturgy. Today reflecting on the significance of liturgy, Cyprian explains, "In the Rule of Benedict, *'opus dei'* means 'the work of God', and the work of God is the liturgy. ... Nothing is to be preferred to the work of God. ... You don't lightly avoid going to choir, you come. And I've tried to live that way, you know, even if it meant that I didn't get much sleep, I'm going to get up and go, because that's what a monk should do. He should be there, at the liturgy. And it should be a major part of our life. ... A Benedictine is supposed to take part in the prayers, but it's supposed to be done beautifully." It is clear that his ardor remains strong.

This strong recommendation of the beautiful liturgies of St. Meinrad fueled Clarence's determination to visit, but his parents were not as enthusiastic about St. Meinrad, at least not at first. This was the Jim Crow era, and St. Meinrad was located south of the Mason-Dixon line in Indiana, a place known to have active Klansmen. They feared for their son's safety. Even though Washington, D.C. was also segregated at the time, segregation in the South was much more extreme. But again they relented, allowing their son to take the long train ride to Louisville, Kentucky on his own, where he would be met by a priest and escorted to St. Meinrad. It was during that first week-long visit that Clarence first saw "Blacks Only" and "Whites Only" signs. While this was troubling, the monks at St. Meinrad were kind, and by the end of the week Clarence had made friends with several. And there were already two black brothers there, so Clarence would not have been the first (although he was the first to stay and the first Black to be ordained a monk at St. Meinrad, as both brothers left the monastery soon thereafter). At the end of that visit, Abbot Ignatius Esser asked Clarence if they would see him again at St. Meinrad. St. Meinrad was, indeed, open to blacks and would welcome him. That visit changed his life forever. Yes, the monks of St. Meinrad would definitely see Clarence again.

"I figure it was my mother." – Fr. Cyprian Davis, O.S.B.

After spending his first year of college at Catholic University (figure 2), Clarence's parents agreed to allow him to enter St. Meinrad in the fall of 1950. Cyprian laughed freely as he recalled those early years. "My novice master [Meinrad Hoffman] thought I didn't know how to work," said Cyprian with a grin. The young Washingtonian was in fact unaccustomed to hard manual labor although he did deliver newspapers to many Howard University professors who lived in his neighborhood. Working in the monastery gardens aggravated his asthma, "One more excuse [not to work]!" said Father Hoffman. Cyprian laughed as he remembered that story. Hoffman, according to Fr. Cyprian, "wanted a black, but he wanted a good one! And he wasn't sure about me!" The novice master, however, got along well with Mrs. Davis, who took the blame for her son's lack of skill with manual labor. "My mother said, 'I explained to him that it was my fault, that I didn't teach you how to work.'" When asked, "What convinced the novice master to allow you to continue?," Cyprian laughingly replied, "I figure it was my mother!" (figure 3).

Figure 2: Young Clarence with a friend at Catholic University in Washington, D.C. (printed with permission of St. Meinrad Archives)

Figure 3: Cyprian with picture of his mother, Evelyn Davis (photo taken by Kimberly Flint-Hamilton)

Davis remembers that the second part of the novitiate was easier than the first. But there were still challenges. Novice master Hoffman believed in humility, repeatedly demanding of young Clarence, "What do you have to be proud of?" When we asked what behaviors Hoffman was interpreting as prideful, Davis' smile saddened just a tiny bit. "I think, in a certain sense, [he] was dealing with me as a black. It was some of that, but I certainly was his first one. And I got through it. I wasn't sure I was going to make it, but I did."

Even though St. Meinrad was open to blacks, southern Indiana was a hard place for a young black man to be in the 1940s and 1950s. Despite the good intentions of the Abbot, it still would take a long time for the culture to change. When Clarence entered the monastery in 1950, the other seminarians were still bemoaning the fact that black minstrel shows had discontinued the year before. An elderly monk who had returned to St. Meinrad didn't know what to make of his new young black brother. He kept asking Clarence "Who *are* you?" and Clarence would answer "I'm a novice" or "I'm going to be a priest." Not getting to the kind of answer he was really seeking, the monk finally demanded, "What ARE you?" It was clear then what he wanted to know. Clarence answered "I'm a Negro." To which the elderly monk answered "What will you DO?" Clarence insisted he would become a priest, and say Mass and all the other things priests do. Well, a Black monk and priest of St. Meinrad would be a first for this senior monk and many others as well. Cyprian with humor in his tone told us that after this frank conversation whenever the elderly monk would see Cyprian he would greet him saying, *"Nigra sum sed formosa!"* (I am black but beautiful!).[3] Clarence took this and much more in stride keeping his focus on his dream to become a priest and live the monastic life ordered by liturgy. It was all worth it to him.

---

[3] Song of Songs 1:5.

"You should remember that very few people have what you have, namely the ability to fulfill your dreams." – Wife of a Howard University Professor

Clarence finally became Cyprian when he took he made his first vows at the end of his novitiate. Novices were allowed to submit a list of three names for the Abbot to consider but they knew it was possible that the Abbot might select a name that was not their list. Hoping his wish would be granted, Clarence purposefully put the name Cyprian on his list. It was of course the name of an African bishop, the martyr St. Cyprian, Bishop of Carthage ca. 248-258.[4] He was very pleased to publically announce his new name, Cyprian, at his profession ceremony (figure 4).

---

[4] Kevin Knight (editor), "St. Cyprian of Carthage", *New Advent Catholic Encyclopedia* (2009), http://www.newadvent.org/cathen/04583b.htm (accessed 5 September 2010). It is important to note that the Abbot did not have to use a name that a novice submitted, but he almost always selected the candidate's first choice.

Figure 4: Cyprian reading Profession Charter at end of novitiate. Note Cyprian's hairstyle in the distinctive monastic "corona."
(printed with permission of St. Meinrad Archives)

In 1954, Cyprian made his profession of solemn vows and in 1956, he was ordained a priest, the first black priest of the Archabbey of St. Meinrad in Indiana (figures 5-7).

Figure 5: Ordination
(printed with permission of St. Meinrad Archives)

To Walk a Path, To Be Transformed, And To Transform   39

Figure 6: Class of 1956
(photo taken by Steven Hamilton from wall photo)

Figure 7: Rev. Cyprian Davis, O.S.B.
(detail of Figure 6)

In reflecting on those years, Cyprian remarked with solemn gratitude, "I've never regretted living this vocation. There were times perhaps when I did think perhaps about leaving, but not really ... I remember when I was young, had just been ordained. The wife of one of the professors at Howard [University], she was not Catholic. She said, 'You should remember that very few people have what you have, namely the ability to fulfill your dreams.'" Cyprian remembered his happiness at having been told that he would teach, and in the fall of 1956 he was sent to the Catholic University of America to earn his Licentiate in Sacred Theology (STL). Another of his dreams was coming to pass. In characteristic modesty he denied that he had any special skills saying, "I'm not nearly as intelligent as my father." But his eyes lit up when he recalled his years at the University of Louvain in Belgium (1958-1963), the first monk from St. Meinrad selected to study at the premier institution. For five years he studied the *familia*, the non-monks, who lived and worked at the medieval Abbey of Cluny, for his master's degree. Cyprian reflected "My work in the Middle Ages is the work of the little people." The *familia* included all the people associated with monastery who were not monks, including serfs, various types of servants, and workers. Without them the monasteries could not exist but they rarely were the focus of historical attention. But, these "little people" and the significant roles they played fascinated Cyprian and ultimately would prepare him for his work on the history of Black Catholics. In many ways Black Catholics have historically been the *familia* of the Catholic Church in the United States.

The years at Louvain were happy ones for Cyprian. While there he served as chaplain for the Benedictine nuns at St. Gertrude and became great friends with them (figure 8). He recalled these sisters as especially kind and intellectually engaging. He also made friends among the diverse student body of Louvain and studied with great historians. When it came time to go home in 1963, he was happy and ready to return but the home he left would be radically different from the one he left in 1958. The United States was in the midst of the Civil Rights movement and the Roman Catholic Church in the middle of the

Second Vatican Council (Vatican II began in 1962 and ended in 1965). Both church and society were undergoing profound changes and he would meet all these changes one way or another.

Figure 8: Cyprian with Abbess for the Benedictine nuns at St. Gertrude, Louvain (printed with permission of St. Meinrad Archives)

Cyprian remembered, "I arrived back here in 1963, in August, in Washington, D.C., within a week of when Martin [Luther King, Jr.] made his famous speech, 'I Have a Dream.'" Cardinal O'Boyle was there at the march, as was the Abbot of the English Benedictine Abbey. Cyprian marched with them. "What I realized was that, I left the United States a proper Negro, but came back with the change that had occurred, realizing it was the Civil Rights movement. ... [When I] got back to St. Meinrad, the change had come there too." Cyprian laughingly called this period between 1963 and 1968 his "discovering that I am black" period.

Parishes, particularly black parishes, invited him to speak and to celebrate Mass (figure 9). He began to consider the question, "why should a black become a Catholic?" His decision to study Medieval Europe involved more than his love for the period. It was also in part to avoid the unpleasant realities of American slavery and historic racism, which he was now having to confront in this turbulent new era.

Figure 9: Celebrating Mass at St. John Church in Evansville, IN
(printed with permission of St. Meinrad Archives)

"We're leaving tonight." – Fr. Camillus Ellsperman, O.S.B.

For five years Cyprian continued to teach at St. Meinrad as the Civil Rights movement pressed on (figures 10-12). When Dr. Martin Luther King, Jr. called on all clergy to join him at Selma, Alabama in 1965, Cyprian did not expect he would be one to answer this call. But he did when he agreed to join another monk,

Fr. Camillus Ellspermann, O.S.B. on a trip South to join the demonstrations in Selma. "He came up to me one day, and he says, 'I'm going to Selma, I've gone to the Abbot, he's given me permission, and I've got a car. We're leaving tonight." Although reluctant at first, he thought, "How am I going to let him go alone? This white man?" Without any more thinking, Cyprian took his place in the car with Fr. Camillus, two other white monks, and a black Baptist minister from Evansville, Indiana. They arrived in Selma the same day the Unitarian minister was shot and killed.[5] They stayed in the Black Catholic parish in Selma for almost a week, and were there when President Lyndon B. Johnson announced he would press on to pass the Civil Rights Act of 1965. This was a turning point in Davis' life. He said, "I had become black."

"Those who are really scholarly are always open and very generous." – Fr. Cyprian Davis, O.S.B.

By 1968, Davis had convinced the Abbot to allow him to return to Louvain to begin working on his Ph.D. He wanted to continue his work on the Abbey of Cluny. But Cyprian's new sense of blackness made him aware that the history of Black Catholics had been virtually ignored. For the Ph.D., Cyprian had to identify a secondary area in which to conduct research. He knew he had his secondary thesis when Brother David Spalding, CFX, author of "The Negro Catholic Congresses, 1889-1894" published in *The Catholic Historical Review* in 1967, gave him all of the research materials he had used to write this article.[6] Regarding Spalding, Cyprian expressed admiration and gratitude. Spalding practiced what Cyprian believes and that is that "those who are really scholarly are always open and very generous." Although Cyprian was not called upon to do the second thesis, this research cache served as his first

---

[5] Reverend James J. Reeb was the Unitarian Universalist minister who assassinated that day while participating in a demonstration.
[6] Later Brother David Spalding would return to his given name and was from then on known as Brother Thomas Spalding, CFX.

Figures 10-12: Cyprian teaching at St. Meinrad
(printed with permission of St. Meinrad Archives)

major lead in pursuing the history of Black Catholics in the United States.

"And this was one of those times!" – **Fr. Cyprian Davis, O.S.B.**

Before returning to Louvain, however, Cyprian experienced yet another life-shaping event. Shortly after the assassination of Martin Luther King Jr. and the rioting that erupted in many major American cities as a response, the Midwest Catholic Clergy Conference met in Detroit. During this meeting black priests and brothers convened *en masse* for the first time ever and initiated what would become the Black Catholic Clergy Caucus. It was a radical move. Most of the priests there had serious complaints, some shared their personal trials as priests, some passionately and loudly, while others focused on the ill treatment of Blacks in the Catholic Church. Some believed that the non-violent way of King had failed and that it was time to begin thinking as Malcolm X. Cyprian's face showed a troubled expression when he recalled this first meeting of the Black Catholic Clergy Caucus in 1968. Acknowledging that many black priests and brothers had had bad experiences in the Church, his own life as a Catholic priest and monk had been quite good. The Benedictines at St. Meinrad had been supportive of Cyprian. He had been living his dream. "I couldn't complain at St. Meinrad. They had sent me away to school, they'd given me an education I'd never have been able to get." At the end of that first Caucus meeting the priests signed a manifesto that had ten points, the first of which was 'The Catholic Church in America is a white racist institution.' Cyprian recalled his thoughts at that pivotal moment. "How can the Spouse of Christ be a white racist institution? ... What was flashing in my mind was, this is just like the French Revolution! ... I'm thinking to myself as we were standing in line, 'what will my Abbot say?' But then it came to me. If my Abbot says anything, I'm going to say, 'you must understand that Catholic Church historians normally will say that, at times that the Catholic Church in its history *was* corrupt, was even moribund! ... And this was one of those times!'" Then Cyprian laughed playfully, recalling that when he returned to St. Meinrad, the Abbot never mentioned the manifesto. "The Abbot had glaucoma, so he didn't read much!" From that time on Cyprian became an active member of the Black Catholic Clergy Caucus and he has rarely missed an annual meeting.

Recalling the years he spent working on his dissertation, Cyprian's expression grew pained when he told us about learning from a fellow student that one of the members of his committee didn't think he was a serious enough scholar. This experience is one that most if not all Black scholars have faced and we winced inwardly remembering our own similar battles with colleagues and committee members who failed to support us. This revelation caused Cyprian to begin to doubt himself. He said, "All of a sudden I thought, I'll never make it. I can never make it. If this guy is after me ... he could scuttle me right away. I've got to go back and do everything *again*." Davis spent years going through all the sources he had reviewed years earlier for his master's degree, making sure that no stone was left unturned. "I began to get depressed," he recalled. "I told the Abbot that I was a little bit depressed, but I did not want him to think I was really depressed, because he would say, 'well it's about time you came back.' ... I'd built it up so much that I thought if I don't make this, I'll have let down the race!" He also did not want to let his brother monks at St. Meinrad down as they had invested so much in him and his education. So he turned his doubts and fears into fuel to give everything he had to the dissertation and making it the best it could be. In 1977 he defended his dissertation in French in Louvain with friends in the audience encouraging him as faced the questions put forth by the jury. When he concluded his argument, the jury stood and applauded his work – not quite the *une grande distinction avec applaudissment* that would have marked the highest level of achievement, but a good-natured applause for all the hard years he had spent on the doctorate. At last, he had earned his doctorate in historical science from the University of Louvain, he had accomplished what the monks at St. Meinrad had supported him in doing, and he had not let down the race (figure 13).

Figure 13: Cyprian holding Ph.D. diploma from University of Louvain
(photo taken by Kimberly Flint-Hamilton)

"If there are human beings, there are records."
Fr. Cyprian Davis, O.S.B.

At Louvain Cyprian had learned to be a historian and to use the historical method expertly. Louvain's philosophy was that "a historian is a historian" and consequently a historian should be able to study, research and write history from any period or culture and do a good job. This preparation and conviction served him well as he commenced the research and writing of *The History of Black Catholics in the United States*, a project that C. Eric Lincoln and Lawrence Mamiya invited him take up as part of a major study on the Black Church funded by the Lilly Foundation in the 1980s. Cyprian told them he was interested but that he did not know if he could get the time to do the research and he would need the permission of his Abbot. Mamiya and Lincoln told him to write a proposal and a budget. In the meantime, the Abbot gave permission and support. When Cyprian heard back from Mamiya and Lincoln, they told him he had not asked for enough money. With a sabbatical and funding, Cyprian had a year to travel around the United States and to Rome to use archives and other sources to begin uncovering the lives, experiences, contributions and faith of

Black Catholics in the United States from the 16th century forward. To do this work that he knew so many Black Catholics desired to have, he used every skill he learned at Louvain. Now he was working in his "secondary" area, Black Catholic history, and his "primary" area, medieval monasticism, proved priceless. He knew how to dig for sources and how to scour them when found them. He knew how to place the subjects of history in their own times, places, and contexts. Cyprian remembered asking Monsignor John Tracy Ellis, the dean of American Catholic history, about where he should look to find historical records of Black Catholics, but Monsignor Ellis merely lamented how sad it was that no sources existed to write a proper history of Black Catholics. Cyprian knew this was not the case because he had also learned at Louvain, "If there are human beings there are records."

Among the most important places his historical excavations took him were to use the sacramental records of St. Augustine, Florida and to the Vatican Archives. Cyprian was especially lucky to be able to use archives of the Apostolic Delegation in Washington, D.C. They had not been long deposited and were being processed when he arrived in the Vatican Archives. Though these papers were in process, the archivist told Cyprian he could look at anything up until 1922. There he found two thick folders filled with documents about the condition of Blacks in the United States.[7]

Cyprian's transition into research and writing Black Catholic history was stoked by the questions that Black Catholics started asking him in the 1960s after he returned from his first years of study at Louvain. When he would visit Black parishes, fundamentally the people wanted to know "What is our history in the Church?" Their questions became his as well. He could not answer them at the time but his training as a historian made it possible for him to begin answering them. When *The History of Black Catholics in the United States* was published in 1990 by Crossroads, it offered what so many Black Catholics had been

---

[7] Eng, *Conversations in the Abbey*, p. 18.

waiting for – the opportunity to understand from a historical point of view their ancestors' places in and contributions to the Catholic Church. And, the invitation that Cyprian gave for others to join in furthering the recovery of Black Catholic history in every chapter of the book helped to generate a new field in Catholic Studies, historical studies of Black Catholics in the United States. Currently, Cyprian is working on an updated edition of *The History of Black Catholics in the United States* that among several new things will include a deeper look at the participation and leadership of Black Catholics in the Civil Rights movement and the role of Black Catholics in the fine and creative arts and popular culture in America.

"I always had wanted to go to Africa and presumed I would never get there." – Fr. Cyprian Davis, O.S.B.

Just as Cyprian did not anticipate how central writing and teaching Black Catholic history would become in life as a scholar and teacher, he also had no idea that another of his childhood dreams would come true in his later years. While he was a child reading histories of Europe he also read about Africa. He was fascinated by Africa and wanted to go there very much. However, because he had not joined a missionary order he thought he would never travel to Africa. In the 1990s Benedictine and Trappist communities in West Africa were seeking a monk/professor to come and teach the young monks the foundations of the Sacred Sciences. This is how another of Cyprian's dreams came true. Between 1990 and 2001, he made five trips to different West African Benedictine and Trappist communities to teach but also to learn. These experiences in the African monasteries had a tremendous positive effect on Cyprian. He said, "I learned a lot. They [the young monks] would come and talk." They told him about life in Africa, about African customs, about their families. They also liked to listen about America. Cyprian taught the monks about the African roots of Christian monasticism about which they knew little. Cyprian was impressed by the "toughness" of monastic life in Africa and the happy devotion he felt in these monasteries. In Africa the monks knelt for prayers on stone floors and went without the luxury of hot water for bathing. Yet and still, they were happy and seemed "carefree." Cyprian remarked, "I appreciated it in the sense that everyone was happy." He also deeply appreciated the great concern they showed for each other and for him. He felt at home in Africa and when he was given keys to libraries in the African monasteries, and he got to learn about Africa from African sources. Much like his first experience of the Catholic Mass, Cyprian fell in love with Africa and he hopes that he will get to visit there again. Reflecting on the time he spent driving alone, avoiding snakes, and getting used to the strange and wonderful environment, Cyprian commented, "There was danger as well as happiness, admiration. But it was living life at its fullest!"

"She was very Catholic – she suffered a lot."
Fr. Cyprian Davis, O.S.B.

We ended the day discussing the history of the Institute for Black Catholic Studies (IBCS), which is celebrating its thirtieth anniversary this year. Both the IBCS and the BCTS grew out of those first meetings of the Black Catholic scholarly community at the Motherhouse of the Oblate Sisters of Providence in 1978 and 1979. Cyprian recalled the efforts of Frs. Joseph Nearon, Thaddeus Posey, and James Lyke (who would soon become Archbishop Lyke). He reflected on the illness and untimely death of Nearon, and on the efforts of Archbishop Lyke, who, as a black archbishop, was the most vocally and materially supportive of Black Catholics. Lyke was instrumental in the production of the African American hymnal, *Lead Me, Guide Me*.[8] He was also supportive of Cyprian's work on the history of Black Catholics. And Lyke strongly advocated for the formation of a scholarly group centered on the history, spirituality, and experiences of Black Catholics. That group would eventually become the BCTS, which began meeting regularly in 1990.

---

[8] *Lead Me, Guide Me: African American Catholic Hymnal* (Chicago, IL: G.I. A. Publications 1987)

The IBCS, however, formed very soon after that first meeting at the Motherhouse. Cyprian recalled the efforts of Dr. Sr. Thea Bowman, F.S.P.A., with the young Institute. He smiled as he recalled how the vibrant, joyful young woman would sometimes burst suddenly into song. "She was very Catholic – she suffered a lot." Her passing in 1990 was a great loss to us all (figure 14).

Figure 14: Cyprian with Sr. Thea Bowman, F.S.P.A.
(printed with permission of St. Meinrad Archives)

The morning after our day interviewing, we met Cyprian the St. Meinrad library to visit the archives. There we hoped to find pictures of Cyprian as a novice and young monk. Cyprian had the keys to the archives so getting in was easy for us. But it makes perfect sense that he should have the keys because for the past forty-seven years he has been the Archabbey's archivist. He is also the archivist for the Swiss-American Congregation of Benedictines, for the National Black Catholic Clergy Caucus, and for the Black Catholic Theological Symposium. The time in the archives was just plain fun. We thoroughly enjoyed ourselves there. There is nothing like being in the archives with an enthusiastic and dedicated archivist who takes pride in his or her place. This is definitely true of Cyprian.

Cyprian has a great collection of photographs that document his life at St. Meinrad from his novitiate to much more recent days. Cyprian's appearance has changed over the years – that's true for all of us! – but what remains consistent in his pictures from entering the St. Meinrad until today is his sincere smile. Whether you are looking at pictures of Cyprian as a novice, saying an Mass outdoors in the 1970s, on stage teaching with Sr. Thea Bowman, F.S.P.A., teaching at the IBCS or attending a BCTS meeting there is a sense of peace, happiness, and contentment comes through in the images.

The most important document Cyprian showed us that day was his profession charter (figures 15-16). Every monk must make a profession charter when he enters the monastery. Cyprian told us that no matter whether the man remains a monk or not, his profession charter is always kept forever in the archives of the monastery as permanent reminder that he was there. Cyprian also told us that when a monk dies, his profession charter is placed on his casket during the funeral. Before the burial that profession charter is removed and returned to the archives to mark for history that he was there. Each profession charter is exactly the same because the words of profession are the same for every profession charter. But, each is perfectly unique because they are they are all hand lettered and decorated, with the first letter of the profession charter *I* being illuminated. The variety of colors and symbols and lettering styles the monks choose makes each profession charter a unique work of art and prayer. Cyprian graciously allowed us to photograph his profession charter and to publish it with this article. It is a beautiful symbol of the life that Cyprian has happily lived now for more than 60 years since he entered St. Meinrad in 1950.

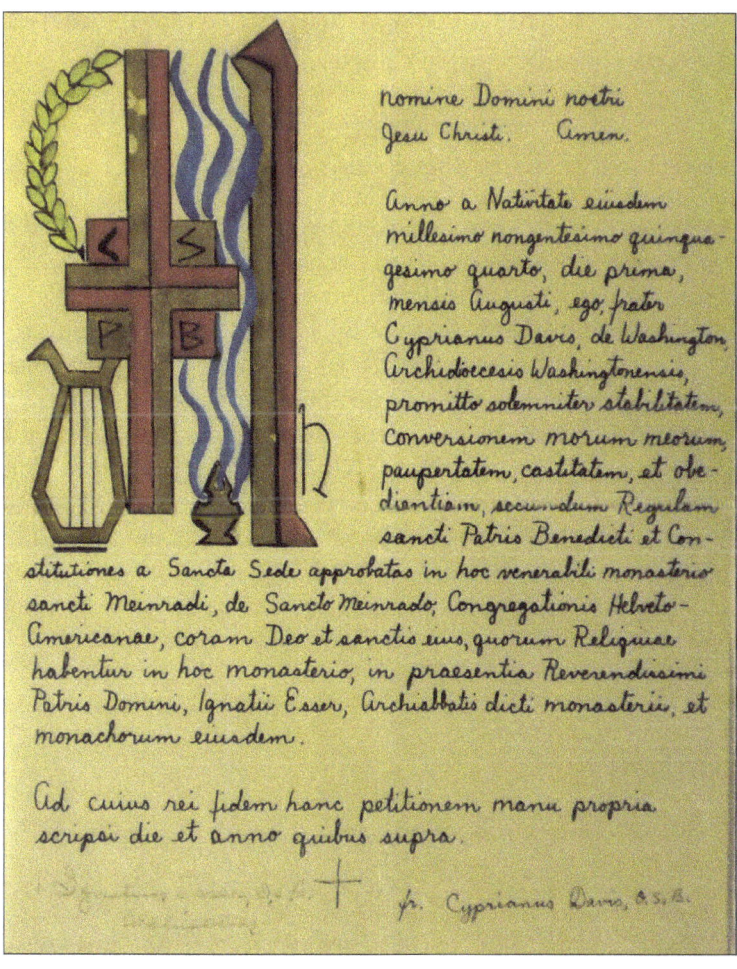

Figure 15: Profession Charter[9] (printed with permission of St. Meinrad Archives)

---

[9] Cyprian made the following comment on the language of the Rule of St. Benedict:
"The Rule of St. Benedict is written in late Latin. Words are used in the Rule that are bad grammar for a classical scholar. This is the case of *conversatio* in the text of the profession. Later monks corrected what they thought was bad Latin. They considered *conversatio* as the same as *conversio*.
Benedictine scholars now insist that *conversatio* is the correct reading. But just what is the meaning of *conversatio*? Most consider that it means "way of life" Something that is stronger than conversion with the stress on perseverance. Because of this, since my profession, *conversio* has reverted to a more ancient

Translation of Profession Charter:

In the name of our Lord Jesus Christ, Amen.

In the year one thousand nine hundred fifty four from his Nativity, on the first day of the month of August, I, brother Cyprian Davis, from Washington, of the Washington Archdiocese, solemnly promise stability, conversion of life (morals, character), poverty, chastity, and obedience, after the Rule of our Holy Father Benedict and the Constitutions approved by the Holy See in this venerable monastery of Saint Meinrad, from Saint Meinrad, of the Swedish American Congregation, before God and his saints, whose relics are held in this monastery, in the presence of the Most Reverend Father, Lord (Dom) Ignatius Esser, Archabbot of the aforesaid monastery, and his monks.

I have written this petition in my own hand in good faith, on which day and year (are noted) above.

Ignatius Esser, O.S.B.
Archabbot

Brother Cyprian Davis, O.S.B.

---

word. In fact, a few other Latin words have reverted back to an earlier text." (personal communication, September 12, 2010).

Figure 16: Detail of Profession Charter
The initials C, S, P, and B stand for: crux sanctissimi Patris Benedicti (trans: the cross of our most Holy Father Benedict)
(printed with permission of St. Meinrad Archives)

After we had photographed and scanned some of the archival documents, Cyprian walked us to our cars and we said our goodbyes. It was nearly noon, time for the monks' midday prayer. Cyprian, however, spent a few minutes with us patiently, thanking us for the time we had spent with him and seeing us on our way. His smile was warm and the day was growing hot. It was already nearly 100° F, and we were eager to get back on the road to our respective homes in our air-conditioned cars. The heat of the day did not seem to affect Cyprian, however. As we drove away, he stood waving to us, smiling, with that twinkle in his eye that we have grown to love. His kindness, hospitality, modesty and grace stayed with us for a long time as we drove away, eager to see him again in October (figure 17).

Figure 17: Cyprian receives honorary doctoral degree from the
University of Notre Dame
Abbot Lambert, Sr. Jamie Phelps O.P., Cyprian Davis O.S.B., Evelyn Davis,
Shawn Copeland, Sr. Eva Regina Martin
(printed with permission of St. Meinrad Archives)

The Role of the Black Catholic Theologian and Scholar in Today's Context[1]

M. Shawn Copeland
Boston College

Based on her keynote address delivered during the 2009 Annual Meeting at Atlanta University's Lyke Center, Copeland takes a look back at the nearly forty-year history of black theological scholarship, reminding us of the intimate link between culture, history, and the ongoing and critical need for a theology that is authentic and responsive to the needs of the poor and marginalized. She reminds us of the urgency for the pursuit of truth and freedom, especially for black scholars and theologians. However, the quest for authenticity comes with a price.

> ...good theology is not abstract but concrete, not neutral but committed. Why? Because the poor were created for freedom and not for poverty.[2]

For the first time in the history of the Catholic Church in the United States, there is a cadre of formally educated theological scholars, women and men of African-American descent—canon lawyers, ethicists, moral theologians, historians, religious educators, sociologists and anthropologists of religion, and systematic theologians.[3] The advocacy for such a group, although

---

[1] This essay is a revision of the opening address of the 20th annual meeting of the Black Catholic Theological Symposium given in at Lyke House, Atlanta, Georgia, October 8, 2009 and draws on material included in the Parks-King Lecture given at Yale Divinity School, New Haven, Connecticut, on February 24, 2009.
[2] James H. Cone, *Black Theology and Black Power*, 2nd Printing (Maryknoll, NY: Orbis Books, 1997), "Preface to the 1989 Edition," xiv.
[3] Augustus Tolton generally is acknowledged as the first African American Catholic priest but, prior to his ordination, there were three others: the Healy brothers—James Augustine, Sherwood, and (Jesuit) Patrick. Sons of an enslaved black woman and an Irish Catholic planter, these men had been isolated by their father's money from the most vicious brunt of racism. But, this left them with little explicit (black) race identification and consciousness. Sherwood Healy was, more than likely, the first Catholic theologian of African descent. A canon lawyer and theologian, he served as a theological *peritus* or expert to Boston's Bishop

sunk deep in the historic nineteenth century struggle of black Catholics to enjoy and exercise full membership in the church, may be traced as well to the response of black Catholic Blessed Sacrament priest and Scripture scholar Joseph Nearon, S.S.S. At the invitation of officers of the Catholic Theological Society of America (CTSA), Nearon made a study of black theology and prepared a report that pressed the "absolute necessity [of] a corps of competent black Catholic theologians,"[4] who would develop a theology accountable to the exigencies of being *black* and *Catholic*.

Yet, a number of external factors and forces shape this scholarly and theological task as well as the context within which it is undertaken. Here, in no particular order, are seven such factors: *First*, most tenured black Catholic theologians began their graduate studies in the late 1970s and early 1980s, just as the discipline faced up to paradigm change in response to historical, social, and pastoral impulses stirred by the Second Vatican Council.[5] In the post-conciliar period, theology has experienced a

---

John Joseph Williams with whom he reportedly traveled to the Second Plenary Council of Baltimore in 1866 and to the First Vatican Council in Rome in 1870 (Albert S. Foley, S.J., "U. S. Colored Priests: Hundred-Year Survey." *America* 89 [13 June 1953]).

[4] Joseph Nearon, S.S.S., "A Challenge to Theology: The Situation of American Blacks." *CTSA Proceedings* 30 (1975): 177-202, especially, 201, idem., "Preliminary Report: Research Committee for Black Theology," CTSA *Proceedings* 29 (1974): 413-417; idem., "The Question of the Church," 7-14, in *Theology: A Portrait in Black*, ed. Thaddeus Posey OFM (Pittsburgh, PA: Capuchin Press, 1988); also see Preston N. Williams, "Religious and Social Aspects of Roman Catholic and Black American Relationships." CTSA *Proceedings* 28 (1973): 15-30.

[5] Between roughly 1930-1950, academic theologians in Europe, particularly in France, began to find neo-Scholastic theology, which had been regnant since Leo XIII's 1879 promulgation of the encyclical *Aeterni Patris*, incapable of responding to the challenges of encroaching secularization in society. For these theologians, principally the Dominicans of Le Saulchoir and the Jesuits of the Lyon Province, theology necessarily involved a "creative hermeneutical exercise in which the sources of Christian faith were reinterrogated with new questions," Marcellino D'Ambrosio, "Ressourcement Theology, Aggiornamento, and the Hermeneutics of Tradition." Communio Vol. 18 (Winter 1991): 530. *Aeterni Patris* ("On the Restoration of Christian Philosophy") dismissed contemporary

fundamental shift *from* the preeminence of scholastic metaphysics in systematics and the manual tradition in ethics *to* ideological criticism in the forms of critiques of domination, critical theories of race, critical race theory, cultural theory, postmodernism, postcolonialism. Further, under the press of *historical consciousness*,[6] of *cultural change*,[7] of widespread *social* (i.e., economic, political, technological) *disorder*[8] and of *religious breakdown*,[9] theology has been challenged to reevaluate its presuppositions, tasks, sources, and methods. Political and liberation theologies undertook the critique of domination, focusing on particularity and the differentiated experience of different human beings, experience as a point of departure and uncovering tensions between the particular and the universal, the normative and situational in hermeneutics. Contextual theologies turned their attention to cultural analyses, although at times referring to aspects of the critique of domination. But, since the late 1990s, theology has turned toward a form of *ressourcement* known as radical orthodoxy; its key features include critiques of modern secularism and liberalism, a rejection of analogy.[10]

---

developments in philosophy and restored neo-scholasticism as the dialogue partner of theology *via* the study of Thomas Aquinas. For a thorough discussion of the implications of the encyclical for the study of Aquinas, see Gerald A. McCool, *Catholic Theology in the Nineteenth Century: The Quest for a Unitary Method* (New York: Seabury, 1977).

[6] Consider these events, which have pressed upon theologizing, namely—the conquest of the so-called 'new world,' centuries of enslavement, the Shoah, enslavement—and these intellectual forces, namely—the Enlightenment, historical critical method in biblical studies, the emergence of cultural studies, the explosion of knowledge, particularly through the internet.

[7] Consider inculturation, shifting cultural customs in relation to economic upward and geographic mobility, the various waves of feminism, changing sexual mores, ethical problems provoked by unbridled technological and genetic manipulation, etc.

[8] Consider the genocides in Eastern Europe as well as in Africa, the deepening conflict and violence between Israelis and Palestinians, the destruction of the World Trade Towers in New York, the war in Iraq, the war in Afghanistan, etc.

[9] Consider the Protestant-Catholic violence in Northern Ireland, Hindu-Islamic violence in India and Pakistan, intra-ethnic dogmatic violence between Sunni and Shia Muslims.

[10] John Milbank and Catherine Pickstock, ed., *Radical Orthodoxy: A New Theology*, (London: Routledge, 1999).

Second, a theology is not only the product of faith but also of a culture. Catholic theologians are challenged not only to acquire knowledge of the culture(s) in which they live and study, write and teach, but also to acknowledge that there exists a "multiplicity of theologies," which may express the one faith.[11] Diversity and pluralism are obvious, if testy, dimensions of life in the United States, and, these tensions characterize our global church.[12]

Third, Christian social ethicist Peter Paris has observed that with the irruption of black theology, "for the first time in the history of religious academe, African Americans [have] a subject matter and a methodological perspective ... peculiarly their own and capable of rigorous academic defense."[13] Yet, that subject matter and perspective has been accorded scant attention in Catholic seminaries, college and university departments of theology.

Fourth, while 'the academy' has become a site of often biting competition for status and prestige, scholars trained in the Humanities are losing this competition to those trained in science, technology, and business.[14] This situation is as disastrous for

---

[11] Bernard Lonergan, *Doctrinal Pluralism* (Milwaukee: Marquette University Press, 1971); idem., *Method in Theology* (New York: Herder and Herder, 1972), 363, 271.

[12] When Pope Paul VI presided over the final session of the Second Vatican Council in 1965, the assembled cardinals and bishops represented and presented, for, perhaps, the first time, a world church. In 1919, the Roman Catholic Church had no bishops of non-European origin, except for the four men belonging to the Indian hierarchy created by Leo XIII in 1896. Both Pius XI and Pius XII were instrumental in widening the racial and cultural diversity of the hierarchy in the twentieth century. The First Synod of African Bishops was held in Rome in 1994, the Second Synod of African Bishops was held in Rome, 4 -25 October 2009.

[13] Peter J. Paris, "Overcoming Alienation in Theological Education," in *Shifting Boundaries: Contextual Approaches to the Structure of Theological Education*, eds. Barbara Wheeler and Edward Farley (Louisville, KY: Westminster/John Knox Press, 1991), 183.

[14] William M. Chace, "The Decline of the English Department: How It Happened and What Could Be Done to Reverse It." *American Scholar* (Autumn 2009), 32-42. Chace documents these shifts by undergraduates in selection of major courses of study: English from 7.6 percent of all majors to 3.9 percent,

science, technology, and business as it is for the Humanities. Human persons are not reducible to atoms or theorems, to statistics or social problems; nor are they reducible to metaphors or attributes, to descriptions or categories. Rather, human persons are instances of the intelligible as intelligent in the world, instances of incarnate moral and ethical choice in a world under the influence of sin, yet standing in relation to a field of supernatural grace.[15]

Fifth, since most black Catholic theologians and scholars have been (and are) trained in European or European-American Catholic educational settings, the exclusion or marginalization of Black Studies in the curriculum may serve to alienate students and faculty of *all* racial-ethnic backgrounds not only from the intellectual fertility of Black Studies but also from the very intellectual ethos of those educational settings. Moreover, for black Catholics, all too often and too easily, such alienation provokes and fuels identity frustration.[16]

Sixth, nearly all black Catholic theologians and scholars teach or work in predominantly white and white Catholic institutions. In this setting, tokenization and trivialization on racial grounds may be all too commonplace. When this is the case, black Catholic theologians and scholars are reduced to a 'colorful' and illustrative slice of social location, while our disciplinary expertise either is diminished and ignored or subordinated to 'racial incidents.' The black theologian and scholar becomes the 'expert' on 'the black

---

Foreign languages and literatures from 2.5 percent to 1.3 percent, Philosophy and religious studies from 0.9 percent to 0.7 percent, History: from 18.5 percent to 10.7 percent, Business from 13.7 percent to 21.9 percent. See also Cornel West, "The Postmodern Crisis of Black Intellectuals," in *Beyond Eurocentrism and Multiculturalism: Prophetic Thought in Postmodern Times,* ed. Cornel West (Monroe, ME: Common Courage Press, 1993), 92-93.
[15] See Bernard Lonergan, *Collected Works of Bernard Lonergan,* Vol. 3, *Insight, A Study of Human Understanding* 5th edition (Toronto: University of Toronto, 1988), 422; idem, "Finality, Love, Marriage," 16-53, in *Collection: Papers by Bernard Lonergan, S. J.,* ed. Frederick E. Crowe (Montreal: Palm Publishers, 1967).
[16] Lonergan, *Insight, A Study of Human Understanding,* 186.

experience' for white colleagues. Yet, if we black Catholic historians, moralists and ethicists, doctrinal and systematic theologians, philosophers and administrators fail to take responsibility for rigorous and sustained research, analysis, and reflection on black experience, we shall deprive our people and the whole church of riches.[17]

And, *finally,* anti-black racism remains an inescapable and lived reality in the United States, even an inescapable and lived reality of Catholic life. Racism does not concern attitudes, feelings, or preferences merely. Rather, racism denotes intentional protracted structured, institutionalized oppression of one race or races by some other race or races. In the United States, either directly or indirectly, racism permeates, deforms, and governs every social, cultural, personal, even, religious encounter or exchange between racialized human subjects.

This list of factors or forces is not exhaustive; however, it does provide a starting point for considering the role of the black

---

[17] For some discussions of the dilemmas, failures, paradoxes, and struggle of the vocation of living the black Catholic scholar—of living a black intellectual life in the United States, see E. Franklin Frazier, "The Failure of the Negro Intellectual." *Negro Digest* (February 1962): 26-36; John Hope Franklin, "The Dilemma of the American Negro Scholar," in *Soon, One Morning, New Writing by American Negroes*, 1940-1962, ed. Herbert Hill (New York: Knopf, 1963), 62-76; Harold Cruse, *The Crisis of the Negro Intellectual: From Its Origins to the Present* (New York: William Morrow & Company, Inc., 1967); Ralph Ellison, "The World and the Jug," in *Shadow and Act*, ed. Ralph Ellison (New York: Random House, 1964), 107-143; Vincent Harding, "The Vocation of the Black Scholar and the Struggles of the Black Community," in *Education and Black Struggle: Notes from the Colonized World* (Cambridge, MA: Harvard Educational Review, 1974), 3-39; Martin Kilson, "Paradoxes of Blackness: Notes on the Crisis of Black Intellectuals," *Dissent* 33 (1986): 70-78; Michele Wallace, *Invisibility Blues: From Pop to Theory* (New York and London: Verso, 1990); bell hooks and Cornel West, *Breaking Bread: Insurgent Black Intellectual Life* (Boston: South End Press, 1991); Jerry Gafio Watts, *Heroism and Black Intellectual Life* (Chapel Hill: University of North Carolina Press, 1994); Cornel West, "The Dilemma of Black Intellectual," *Cultural Critique* 1 (Fall 1985): 132-146; idem, *Race Matters* (Boston: Beacon Press, 1994), Bryan N. Massingale, "Cyprian Davis and the Black Catholic Intellectual Vocation," *U. S. Catholic Historian* 28 (1) (Winter 2010): 65-82.

Catholic theologian and scholar in today's context. Let me frame the remainder of the discussion by adverting to a set of remarks and three conditions: (1) remarks by Pope Benedict XVI in meeting with the academic community of the Czech Republic, (2) the condition of the Church, (3) the condition of black people, and (4) the condition of our country.

Framing The Discussion: Taking Our Bearings

First: During his September 2009 pastoral visit to the Czech Republic, Pope Benedict XVI spoke with members of the academic community—students and professors. The pope identified quite personally with this community and referred to his former member of the professoriate. He presented himself as one who was, "solicitous of the right to academic freedom and the responsibility for the authentic use of reason."[18] Further, the pope observed: "The yearning for freedom and truth is inalienably part of our common humanity. It can never be eliminated; and, as history has shown, it is denied at humanity's own peril."[19] The Czech revolt against totalitarian ideology in 1989 formed the historical, cultural, and political backdrop for his remarks.[20] Benedict decried the fragmentation in contemporary society brought on by "massive growth in information and technology [resulting in the] temptation to detach reason from pursuit of truth," and, thus, surrender to the "lure" of hasty and crude forms of ideology, utilitarianism, relativism, and secularism.[21] Moreover, the pope concluded, commitment to freedom and truth are

---

[18] Pope Benedict XVI, "Meeting with Members of the Academic Community, Address by the Holy Father." 27 September 2009, http://www.vatican.va/holy_father/benedict_xvi/speeches/2009/september/documents/hf_ben_xvi_spc_20090927_mondo-accademico_en.html (accessed July 31, 2010).
[19] Ibid.
[20] This revolt, known as the "Velvet Revolution," refers to the more than six weeks of non-violent demonstrations by citizens of Prague between November 17 and December 29, 1989, which brought down the one-party Communist government.
[21] Pope Benedict XVI, "Meeting with Members of the Academic Community: Address by the Holy Father."

essential in the "human formation" (*paideia*) of the young, to the cultivation of virtue and its incarnation.[22]

Second: The Condition of Our Church: Listen to the words of the Marcan Jesus:

> You know that among the Gentiles those whom they recognize as their rulers lord it over them, and their great ones are tyrants over them. But it is not so among you; but whoever wishes to become great among you must be your servant, and whoever wishes to be first among you must be a slave of all. For the Son of Man came not to be served, but to serve, and to give his life a ransom for many (Mark 10: 42-45).

This familiar passage leapt out from the pages of the final chapter of *What Would Jesus Deconstruct: The Good News of Postmodernism for the Church*.[23] In that chapter, John Caputo analyzes two ecclesial communities—St. Malachy's, a typical Catholic parish in the Archdiocese of Philadelphia, and Ikon, an experiment in spiritual community. On the one hand, Ikon is described as "an independent avant-garde assembly of young laypeople, intellectual, church and community activists, including non-Christians, who all meet in a bar" to read and interpret Sacred Scripture often through dramaturgical performance.[24] St. Malachy's, on the other hand, is

> traditional ministry ... rectory ... weekly schedule of masses and the sacraments, parish committees, a parish school, a parish bulletin, and all the usual outer trappings of institutional life, with a Cardinal Archbishop overseeing the whole operation.[25]

---

[22] Ibid.
[23] John Caputo, *What Would Jesus Deconstruct? The Good News of Postmodernism for the Church* (Grand Rapids, MI: Baker Academic Press, 2007).
[24] Ibid., 137.
[25] Ibid., 129.

The spiritual and liturgical daring of Ikon may excite and entice, but St. Malachy's instantiates the condition of our church not only in the U. S., but also in many places around the globe.

Caputo introduces the condition of the U. S. church through Father John McNamee's book, *The Diary of a City Priest*.[26] Like many of the Catholic parishes left in most inner cities, St. Malachy's sits in the midst of a neighborhood assaulted relentlessly by crime, drugs, squalor, anxiety, fear, and violence. McNamee seems only to want to *accompany* the children, women, and men, who are his parish and to offer them what they need, to nourish them with the bread of eternal life. He charts his spiritual journey and painful discovery of two churches: "the Big, visible one on top," with bishops, power, functional buildings, and money; and the other church, "down in the underbelly of the kingdom of God, in the streets," among the poor and despised, without money and resources because there are few if any Catholics in the parish boundaries.[27] "Two churches," Caputo writes, "the owners of the church, who have all the power, and the working church whose only power is the power of powerlessness that commands our faith."[28]

Beset by spreading scandal, repressed in vision, lost in a labyrinth of power, the Big church crashes against its own Mystery, squandering grace; yet down in the underbelly of the kingdom of God, we had better learn compassion and solidarity, creativity and strategy, humility and courage, prayer and fasting. In other words, we must be "as shrewd as snakes and as innocent as doves" (Matthew 10:16).

Third and *Fourth*: The condition of black people *is* the condition of our country. To put it differently, black people are like the canary used to test the quality of oxygen in a coal mine.

---

[26] John P. McNamee, *The Diary of a City Priest* (Kansas City, MO: Sheed and Ward, 1993).
[27] Cited in Caputo, *What Would Jesus Deconstruct?* 117.
[28] John Caputo, *What Would Jesus Deconstruct?*, 120.

The condition of black people serves as an early warning system, alerting the rest of the country to toxic social policies and programs.

In the final textual paragraph of *Where Do We Go From Here: Chaos or Community*,[29] the Reverend Dr. Martin Luther King, Jr., calls for active, practical commitment to the work of justice in a social order in which black children, women, and men are choked with frustration, hurt, and despair. Although this book was published only a few years following the signing of the Civil Rights Act of 1964, King never confused formal legislation with the difficult reality of reform.[30] In *Where Do We Go From Here*, King reconceived and reinterpreted black power, dissected anti-black racism, clarified questions of black identity, class status, responsibility, and demanded government attention to housing and education and "the total, direct and immediate abolition of poverty."[31] King concluded by setting out strategic priorities: "quality education for all [and] a creative link between parents and schools,"[32] expanded employment, "new methods of civic participation in decision-making,"[33] and housing, which "is too important to be left to private enterprise with only minor government effort to shape policy."[34]

More than four decades later, these same issues—education, poverty and unemployment, democratic participation, and housing—remain unresolved.[35] The grave and deteriorated

---

[29] Martin Luther King, Jr., *Where Do We Go from Here: Chaos or Community?* (New York: Harper & Row, 1967).
[30] Ibid., 5.
[31] Ibid., 166.
[32] Ibid., 195.
[33] Ibid., 200.
[34] Ibid., 202.
[35] During the 2008 presidential campaign, these same issues—education, employment, democratic participation, and housing—proved resonant and compelling. Indeed, in a speech delivered in quest of change, then-candidate Barak Obama in a speech in South Carolina in November 2007 reached back four decades to pull forward that same call to arms, a vision, and hope. See Tim Dickinson, "The Fierce Urgency of Now," *Rolling Stone Magazine*, National Affairs (November 2007).

conditions of New Orleans and Detroit make this abundantly clear. The existential, cultural, and social challenges that these cities and their people face and represent plead for a renewed and critical engagement by black theologians and scholars—indeed all theologians and scholars—with the concrete condition of the poor. King put it this way:

> It is time for the Negro haves to join hands with the Negro have-nots and, with compassion, journey into that other country of hurt and denial. It is time for the Negro middle class to rise up from its stool of indifference, to retreat from its flight into unreality and to bring its full resources—its heart, its mind and its checkbook—to the aid of the less fortunate brother. The salvation of the Negro middle class is ultimately dependent upon the salvation of the Negro masses.[36]

King did not aim "to integrate" blacks into the prevailing values of American society. Rather, he urged blacks to be "those creative dissenters who [would] call ... the nation to a higher destiny, to a new plateau of compassion, to a more notable expression of humanness."[37]

Hurricane Katrina was responsible for the destruction of life and property along the Gulf Coast of Louisiana, Mississippi, and Alabama.[38] Hurricane Katrina uncovered the social suffering

---

[36] King, *Where Do We Go from Here*, 132.
[37] Ibid., 133.
[38] The geographic area affected covers more than 90,000 miles or roughly the size of the state of Oregon. Nearly 1.7 million residents lived in areas that flooded or suffered moderate or catastrophic storm damage. Before Katrina, Mississippi was ranked the second poorest state in the country, Louisiana third, Alabama sixth. Michael Eric Dyson writes, "More than 90,000 people in each of the areas [damaged] by Katrina in Mississippi, Louisiana, and Alabama made less than $10,000 a year. Before the storm, New Orleans, with a 67.9 % black population, had more than 103,000 poor people," in *Come Hell or High Water: Hurricane Katrina and the Color of Disaster* (New York: Basic Books, 2006), 5. In other words, New Orleans had a poverty rate of 23% or 76 % higher than the national average of 13.1 %. In comparison with 290 other large U. S. counties, the Crescent City ranked at seventh in poverty. At the time of the hurricane, the median household income in New Orleans was $31,369, while the national

endured by the poor and poor black people of New Orleans. To borrow a well-known construct from William Jones, here black social suffering was "maldistributed, negative, enormous, and transgenerational."[39] Black social suffering has and has remained massive, public, publicly inflicted, and publicly prolonged by publicly elected representatives of the Republic. Perhaps, change is on the way.

Hurricane Katrina fractured the social set-up, that is, the historical, religious, cultural, social institutions and patterns of daily living. But the fracture was long in the making, the vulnerability of that set-up may be charged to federal policies, particularly, those policies regarding the racial segregation of public housing.[40] Those who suffered the brutal aftermath of Hurricane Katrina had lived in a toxic concentration of poverty: poor neighborhoods, poor schools, poor paying jobs. Post-industrial urban decline spiced the pot. As David Dante Troutt explains:

> the primary effect of federal housing policy, white flight, urban depopulation, and the rise of low-wage service economy is a deepening isolation and concentration of the urban (particularly black) poor. No longer necessary to a manufacturing sector that generally paid workers well enough to cover mortgages and provide pensions, college tuition, and other facets of middle-class existence, these folk became irrelevant. As their social distance from

---

median household income stood at $44,684. Twenty-nine percent of blacks in New Orleans lived below the 2005 poverty threshold of $19, 157 for a family of four. New Orleans out ranked the national average of elders with disabilities at roughly 57 % [national average: 39.6 %] and Louisiana's black population [31.5] accounted for 69 % of all children in poverty. Before Hurricane Katrina, 44 % of all black men sixteen and older were jobless (United States Department of Health and Human Services, The 2005 HHS Poverty Guidelines http://aspe.hhs.gov/poverty/05poverty.shtml, 1 April 2007).
[39] William R. Jones, *Is God A White Racist: A Preamble to Black Theology* (Garden City, NY: Anchor Press/Doubleday, 1973), 21-22.
[40] David Dane Troutt, "Many Thousand Gone, Again," in *After the Storm: Black Intellectuals Explore the Meaning of Hurricane Katrina*, ed. David Dante Troutt (New York: The New Press, 2006), 8.

mainstream life increased with each generation, they grew more culturally distinct (gangster rap); incarceratable (prison industrial complex); unassimilable (Ebonics); pathological (out-of-wedlock birth, infant mortality, and low 'marriageability' rates); labelable ('underclass,' 'looters,' 'playas,' 'hoes,' 'pimps'); and detestable.[41]

The social-set up was structured and dependent upon social oppression. The historic social injustice that poor and poor black people suffer was caused not by tyrannical coercion but as Iris Marion Young writes, "by the everyday practices of a well-intentioned liberal society."[42] These practices are embedded in the epistemic, metaphysical, and moral atmosphere in which such structural oppression in a liberal society takes place. Moreover, they are embedded in and maintained by "unquestioned norms, habits, and symbols, in assumptions underlying institutional rules and the collective consequence of following those rules."[43]

More than a century of 'Jim Crow' laws and customs had denied and/or severely circumscribed black access to educational and skill development. This denial and limitation translated into the protection of white labor and increased profits for white capital. Moreover, *de facto* and *de jure* segregation rules, restrictive covenants, prohibitions on home ownership, discrimination in mortgage lending, and political disenfranchisement conspired further to marginalize black people from meaningful engagement in the social order. The poor and poor black people trapped by the waters of Hurricane Katrina already were powerless because of their fragile economic and social status; now they were accorded little or no dignity and respect.

Hurricane Katrina brutally and swiftly dispatched New Orleans, but Detroit has been battling a rising tide of decay for at

---

[41] Ibid., 7-8.
[42] Iris Marion Young, *Justice and Politics of Difference* (Princeton: Princeton University Press, 1990), 41.
[43] Ibid.

least four decades, and the past twenty years have been bleak, certainly. Six days after Katrina struck, Detroit was cited as the "nation's poorest city, with about one in three residents living below the federal poverty level."[44] According to U. S. Census Bureau reports, 33.6% of Detroiters had income below the poverty level in 2004 compared with 23% in 2002, and 47.8 % of Detroit children lived below the poverty level in 2004, placing Detroit second in that category behind Atlanta.[45] The middle-class, especially those whom King had called the "Negro haves," had left poor people behind.

Writing for *The New York Times* in December 2008, Mary Chapman recorded Congress' stiff and initial rejection of a loan to the automakers and interviewed city residents. Cindy Williams, a waitress at downtown Detroit's American Coney Island restaurant put it trenchantly: "[T]he Big Three *is* Detroit. If the companies don't get money, Detroit is done for."[46] A white suburban attorney and a black community activist both criticized the initial refusal: Jeffrey Schwartz wondered if the "government is for bankers and Wall Street, and then makes the decision not to support [the automobile] industry." Malik Shabazz declared, "Bail out people, not the banks. Give the banks money? No problem. But the car companies, man, they had to do flips, and they didn't get a dime."[47] *New York Times* columnist Bob Herbert contested the preferential option for Wall Street:

---

[44] Patricia Montemurri, Kathleen Gray, and Cecil Angel, "Detroit Tops Nation in Poverty Census," http://www-personal.umich.edu/~gmarkus/montemurri.htm (accessed February 22, 2009).
[45] Ibid. That same year the median household income in Detroit was $27,871 and in the state it was $44,905. Governor Jennifer Granholm pressed for an increase in the hourly minimum wage, which lingered at $5.15. Unemployment in the city hovered around 15%. Kurt Metzger, research director of Wayne State University's Center for Urban Studies put the statistics in real numbers: 75,000 to 80,000 people were living in poverty in the Motor City.
[46] Ibid.
[47] Ibid.

> When the champagne and caviar crowd is in trouble, there is no conceivable limit to the amount of taxpayer money that can be found, and found quickly.
>
> But when it comes to ordinary citizens in dire situations—those being thrown out of work or forced from their homes by foreclosure or driven into bankruptcy because of illness and a lack of adequate health insurance—well, then we have to start pinching pennies.
>
> We can find trillions ... for pompous, self-righteous high-rollers who wrecked their companies and the economy. But what about the working poor and the young people who are being clobbered in this downturn, battered so badly that they're all but destitute? Can we find any way to help them?[48]

The social-set up was structured and dependent upon social oppression. For nearly three decades, Black, Middle Eastern, Polish, and Appalachian workers were forced to fight their way into the automobile factories and into the unions. With the exception of the Ford Motor Company, which used blacks as strikebreakers, only the labor shortages brought on by the Second World War compelled the auto manufacturers to hire blacks in large numbers. But, by ensuring that all superintendents and floor stewards and foremen were white and that 90% of all skilled tradesmen and apprentices were white, the manufacturers cultivated and established 'Jim Crow.' Black, Middle Eastern, and Polish workers were assigned the dirtiest, noisiest, and most dangerous of the factory's jobs in the foundry, body shop, and engine assembly areas. This work required the greatest physical stain as well as regular exposure to poisonous combinations of chemicals and gases. In the period before the federal government's creation of OSHA (Occupational Safety and Health Administration) guidelines, faulty equipment and lax supervision put these workers at literal risk of the loss of limb and life. These

---

[48] Bob Herbert, "Beyond the Fat Cats," *The New York Times*, 10 November 2008, http://www.nytimes.com/2008/11/11/opinion/11herbert.html? (accessed February 22, 2009).

men and women workers had to contend daily with an institution that considered them dispensable; they suffered high rates of hypertension, high blood pressure, and thrombophlebitis.[49]

In one study of the city, *Detroit: I Do Mind Dying*, Dan Georgakas and Marvin Surkin narrate the push back of poor and poor black workers against economic and cultural abuse. And the analyses of James Boggs[50] reflect the thinking of a small group of factory workers, who advanced a "distinctive Marxian critique of the factory as a form of neo-plantation capitalism" in an effort to stimulate new insights about the situation and generate creative imaginative response.[51] In the summer of 1967, Detroit exploded in violent rebellion: frustrated, angry, even self-aggrieved residents looted and burned stores, small businesses, restaurants, and deteriorating homes. The result was not meaningful social change but intensified social oppression and social suffering as businesses and middle- and upper-middle class families left the city for white suburbs.[52]

The neighborhoods of Detroit have never recovered from the 1967 rebellion; the anger and depression was contagious. The center of the city emptied and grew stagnant: Hotels, apartment buildings, specialty clothiers, department stores, book stores, restaurants, and theatres closed.[53] In the late 1970s and early 1980s

---

[49] Dan Georgakas and Marvin Surkin, *Detroit: I Do Mind Dying: A Study of Urban Revolution*, 2nd edition (Cambridge, MA: South End Press, 1998), especially 85-106.
[50] James Boggs, *The American Revolution: Pages from a Negro Worker's Notebook* (1963; New York and London: Monthly Review Press, 1968); idem, *Racism and the Class Struggle: Further Pages from a Black Worker's Notebook* (New York and London: Monthly Review Press, 1970).
[51] Georgakas and Surkin, *Detroit: I Do Mind Dying*, 105.
[52] This rebellion left at least 41 people dead, more than 300 injured, 3,000 arrested, and 5,000 homeless. In the core city, 1,300 burned buildings and 2,700 destroyed businesses totaled $500 million dollars in damage.
[53] The most egregious insult to the city was J. L. Hudson's Department store, the tallest in the country and second only to Macy's anchor store in New York in square footage. The store closed its doors in 1983 and the 2.2 million square foot building of 33 levels sat empty for fifteen years, before being imploded in October 1998. Controlled Demolition, Inc. "J.L. Hudson Department Store"

the automakers along with key developers and the new black mayor's promises ushered in a $350 million complex known as the Renaissance Center with little regard as to how unemployed and underemployed city residents might sustain luxury apartments, offices, hotels, specialty shops, restaurants, and entertainment facilities. The Renaissance Center was a twist for the worse.

The Role of the Black Theologian and Scholar in *Today's* Context

Reflecting on twenty years of rigorous, passionate, committed theology, James Cone closed the preface of the 1989 edition of his *Black Theology and Black Power*[54] with these words: "good theology is not abstract but concrete, not neutral but committed. Why? Because the poor were created for freedom and not for poverty." The year 2009 marks the fortieth anniversary of *Black Theology and Black Power*. This remarkable work, "written in anger and disgust,"[55] in the turbulent aftermath of the murder of the Reverend Dr. Martin Luther King, Jr., was intensely personal and existential, profoundly polemical and prophetic. Cone patterned his understanding of the role of a black theologian by adverting to Amiri Baraka's (LeRoi Jones) description of the work or role or vocation of "all aspiring black intellectuals."[56] That work, Baraka asserted, is "to report and reflect so precisely the nature of the society, that other[s] will be moved by the exactness of [this] rendering."[57] Arguably, this entails the pull and shock of critical interrogation, understanding, and judgment; moreover, for blacks and for whites, for *all* of us in this society, this 'moving' implies self-reflection, conversion, perhaps, *metanoia*.

Historian and socio-cultural analyst Vincent Harding writes

---

http://www.controlled-demolition.com/jl-hudson-department-store (accessed July 31, 2010).
[54] James H. Cone, *Black Theology and Black Power* (New York: Seabury Press, 1969).
[55] Ibid., 3
[56] Ibid.
[57] Ibid.

pointedly and movingly of the vocation of the black scholar.[58] Harding lays down a steely challenge regarding the necessity and soul wrenching integrity of the question of vocation. Despite their "more tastefully [and] delicately wrought walls," the academy, he contends, proves itself ultimately deflecting and unsatisfactory. The black scholar finds the exigencies of her or his vocation in the life and condition of the black community: "It is that community through which vocation, purpose, direction, and life itself are most fully known and lived."[59] The demands of this vocation are, at times, Harding acknowledges, difficult to hear, difficult to admit for our community's history, its colonization, and its rich and jagged culture form:

> an agonizing prism through which to pass the continuous spectrum of our often battered, safety-seeking lives. Nevertheless, if the search for vocation is to be synonymous with the ongoing quest for integrity, we have no other choice. For it is only within the context of the long fight for freedom of the black community that we are ultimately moved towards a true sense of ourselves.[60]

Thus, Harding concludes: "When we ask what it means to be a black scholar to live the truth of black struggle and black hope, it is self-evident that words are not sufficient. Examples are far more to the point."[61] The vocation of the black scholar and theologian involves truth-telling, ideology critique, identifying and confronting all manifestations of crippling self-hatred within, whether within scholars and theologians themselves or within black people. Finally, Harding chides black scholars and theologians to face down personal weakness—not to shirk

---

[58] Harding and his political scientist colleague William Strickland proved to be perceptive advisors to the national staff of the National Black Sisters' Conference (NBSC), a national organization of black Catholic vowed religious women, which, at the time, was headquartered in Pittsburgh, Pennsylvania.
[59] Vincent Harding, "The Vocation of the Black Scholar and the Struggles of the Black Community," in *Education and Black Struggle: Notes from the Colonized World*, ed. Institute of the Black World (Cambridge, Mass.: Harvard Educational Review, 1974): 7.
[60] Ibid.
[61] Ibid., 21.

arduous, unglamorous work, "to be hard" on oneself, to be ruthless with ... personal softness, to discipline [the] mind and [one's] schedule."[62]

The vocation of the black Catholic theologian and scholar in today's context is to live a life of critically engaged scholarship, that is, to contest any attempt to domesticate the Gospel, to retrieve the story of Jesus of Nazareth and clarify it as a 'dangerous memory,'[63] that is, a memory that makes a demand on us, that refuses to succumb to thrall of amnesia, which filters out oppression and social suffering in history and in society. Above all, the vocation of the black scholar and theologian is to tell the truth especially in uncomfortable settings. In poetic injunction, Mari Evans charges black scholars and theologians:

> Speak the truth to the people.
> Talk sense to the people.
> Free them with reason.
> Free them with honesty.
> Free them with Love and Courage and Care
> For their being
> Speak the truth to the people
> To identify the enemy is to free the mind
> Free the mind of the people
> Speak to the mind of the people
> Speak truth.[64]

If black scholars and theologians take up the pursuit of truth and freedom as Pope Benedict XVI urges, then they must make an uncompromising commitment to follow where truth leads and to use freedom responsibly, wisely. If black scholars and theologians take up the pursuit of truth and freedom as Vincent Harding and Mari Evans urge, then they must take themselves and the condition of black people in church and in society seriously. If

---

[62] Ibid., 25.
[63] Johann Baptist Metz, *Faith in History and Society: Toward a Practical Fundamental Theology*, trans. David Smith (New York: Seabury Press, 1980), 109.
[64] Mari Evans, Excerpt from: "Speak The Truth To The People," in *Continuum: New and Selected Poems* (Baltimore, MD: Black Classic Press, 1970), 22-23.

black scholars and theologians speak and act and live in truth, then they will pay a price. For there is a price to paid in devoting disciplined, serious, and imaginative thinking to the condition of black people, in creating and sustaining programs that support authentic liberation, in speaking truth to all people.

WORKS CITED

Boggs, James. *The American Revolution: Pages from a Negro Worker's Notebook*. New York and London: Monthly Review Press, 1968.

--------. *Racism and the Class Struggle: Further Pages from a Black Worker's Notebook*. New York and London: Monthly Review Press, 1970.

Caputo, John. *What Would Jesus Deconstruct? The Good News of Postmodernism for the Church*. Grand Rapids, MI: Baker Academic Press, 2007.

Chace, William M. "The Decline of the English Department: How It Happened and What Could Be Done to Reverse It." *American Scholar* 78(4) (Autumn 2009): 32-42.

Cone, James. *Black Theology and Black Power*. New York: Seabury Press, 1969.

-------. *Black Theology and Black Power, 2nd Printing*. Maryknoll, New York: Orbis Books, 1997.

Controlled Demolition, Inc. "J.L. Hudson Department Store." http://www.controlled-demolition.com/jl-hudson-department-store (accessed July 31, 2010).

Cruse, Harold. *The Crisis of the Negro Intellectual: From Its Origins to the Present*. New York: William Morrow & Company, Inc., 1967.

D'Ambrosio, Marcellino. "Ressourcement Theology, Aggrionamento, and the Hermeneutics of Tradition." *Communio* Vol. 18 (Winter 1991): 530.

Dickinson, Tim. "The Fierce Urgency of Now." *Rolling Stones Magazine, National Affairs* (November 2007).

Dyson, Michael Eric. *Come Hell or High Water: Hurricane Katrina and the Color of Disaster*. New York: Basic Books, 2006.

Ellison, Ralph. "The World and the Jug." In *Shadow and the Act*, ed. Ralph Ellison, 107-143. New York: Random House, 1964.

Evans, Mari. *Continuum: New and Selected Poems.* Baltimore, MD: Black Classic Press, 1970.

Foley, Albert S.J. "U.S. Colored Priests: Hundred-Year Survey." *America* 89 (13 June 1953).

Franklin, John Hope. "The Dilemma of the American Negro Scholar." In *Soon, One Morning, New Writing by American Negroes, 1940-1962*, ed. Herbert Hill, 62-76. New York: Knopf, 1963, 1963.

Frazier, E. Franklin. "The Failure of the Negro Intellectual." *Negro Digest* (February 1962): 26-36.

Georgakas, Dan and Marvin Surkin. Detroit: I Do Mind Dying: A Study of Urban Revolution 2nd ed. Cambridge, MA: South End Press, 1998.

Harding, Vincent. "The Vocation of the Black Scholar and the Struggles of the Black Community." In *Education and Black Struggle: Notes from the Colonized World*, ed. Institute of the Black World, 3-39. Cambridge, MA: Harvard Educational Review, 1974.

Herbert, Bob. "Beyond the Fat Cats." The New York Times, November 10, 2008. http://www.nytimes.com/2008/11/11/opinion/11herbert.html (accessed February 22, 2009).

Hooks, Bell and Cornel West. *Breaking Bread: Insurgent Black Intellectual Life.* Boston: South End Press, 1991.

Jones, William R. *Is God A White Racist: A Preamble to Black Theology.* Garden City, NY: Anchor Press/Doubleday, 1973.

Kilson, Martin. "Paradoxes of Blackness: Notes on the Crisis of Black Intellectuals." *Dissent* (1986): 70-78. http://www.dissentmagazine.org/article/?article=3472 (accessed July 31, 2010).

King, Martin Luther Jr. *Where Do We Go From Here: Chaos or Community?* New York: Harper & Row, 1967.

Lonergan, Bernard. "Finality, Love, Marriage." In *Collection: Papers by Bernard Lonergan, S.J.*, ed. Frederick E. Crowe, 16-53. Montreal: Palm Publishers, 1967.

\------. *Doctrinal Pluralism*. Milwaukee: Marquette University Press, 1971.

\------. *Method in Theology*. New York: Herder and Herder, 1972.

_____. *Collected Works of Bernard Lonergan, Vol. 3, Insight, A Study of Human Understanding* 5th ed. Toronto: University of Toronto, 1988.

Massingale, Bryan N. "Cyprian Davis and the Black Catholic Intellectual Vocation." *U.S. Catholic Historian* 28(1) (Winter 2010): 65-82.

McCook, Gerald A. *Catholic Theology in the Nineteenth Century: The Quest for a Unitary Method*. New York: Seabury, 1977.

McNamme, John P. *The Diary of a City Priest*. Kansas City, MO: Sheed and Ward, 1993.

Metz, Johann Baptist. *Faith in History and Society: Toward a Practical Fundamental Theology* (trans. By David Smith). New York: Seabury Press, 1980.

Milbank, John and Catherine Pickstock, eds. *Radical Orthodoxy: A New Theology*. London: Routledge, 1999.

Montemurri, Patricia, Kathleen Gray, and Cecil Angel. "Detroit Tops Nation in Poverty Census." August 31, 2005. http://www-personal.umich.edu/~gmarkus/montemurri.htm (accessed February 22, 2009).

Nearon, Joseph, S.S.S. "A Challenge to Theology: The Situation of American Blacks." *CTSA Proceedings* 28 (1973): 177-202.

\------. "Preliminary Report: Research Committee for Black Theology." *CTSA Proceedings* 29 (1974): 413-317.

\---------. "The Question of the Church." In *Theology: A Portrait in Black*, ed. Thaddeus Posey O.F.M. Pittsburgh, PA: Capuchin Press, 1980.

Paris, Peter J. "Overcoming Alienation in Theological Education." In *Shifting Boundaries: Contextual Approaches to the Structure of Theological Education*, eds. Barbara Wheeler and Edward Farley, 181-200. Louisville, KY: Westminster/John Knox Press, 1991.

Pope Benedict XVI. "Meeting with Members of the Academic Community, Address by the Holy Father." 27 September 2009, http://www.vatican.va/holy_father/benedict_xvi/speeches/2009/september/documents/hf_ben-xvi_spe_20090927_mondo-accademico_en.html (accessed July 31, 2010).

Troutt, David Dane, ed. *After the Storm: Black Intellectuals Explore the Meaning of Hurricane Katrina.* New York: The New Press, 2006.

Wallace, Michele. *Invisibility Blues: From Pop to Theory.* New York and London: Verso, 1990.

Watts, Jerry Gafio. *Heroism and Black Intellectual Life.* Chapel Hill: University of North Carolina Press, 1994.

West, Cornel. "The Postmodern Crisis of Black Intellectuals." In *Beyond Eurocentrism and Multiculturalism: Prophetic Thought in Postmodern Times*, ed. Cornel West, 92-93. Monroe, ME: Common Courage Press, 1993.

------. "The Dilemma of Black Intellectual." *Cultural Critique* 1 (Fall 1985): 132-146.

------. *Race Matters.* Boston: Beacon Press, 1994.

Williams, Preston N. "Religious and Social Aspects of Roman Catholic and Black American Relationships." *CTSA Proceedings* 28 (1973): 15-30.

Young, Iris Marion. *Justice and Politics of Difference.* Princeton: Princeton University Press, 1990.

"Righteous Discontent:" Black Catholic Protest in the United States of America, 1817-1941

Diane Batts Morrow
University of Georgia

In this essay, based on a paper delivered at the 2009 Annual Meeting at the Atlanta University Center, Morrow shows the awareness of black Catholics about their position within the Catholic Church between the years 1817 and the 1940s and their struggle to improve their situation. Black Catholics from this period show a strong desire to function as agents of positive change in their Church, and to challenge discrimination within their parishes.

Black Catholics in the United States have traditionally advocated their own cause in an essentially Euro-centric institutional Roman Catholic Church, because, as Fr. Cyprian Davis, O.S.B., has aptly observed, "...as was the case with so many of the Catholic clergy at that period, there was little respect for people of African descent, either for their history or for their humanity."[1] Other esteemed scholars of the black Roman Catholic experience have further delineated the problem. Dr. Jamie Phelps, OP has noted:

> "The spiritual traditions of the Catholic church, for example, were transmitted to the sons and daughters of Africa without any consciousness of the cultural specific ways--Spanish, Irish, German, English, French, or Italian--in which they were being transmitted. In addition, these ministers of God's good news sometimes maintained a disdain for the natural religious expression of blacks. For

---

[1] Cyprian Davis, O.S.B., *The History of Black Catholics in the United States* (New York: Crossroad, 1990),133.

them blacks needed to be elevated and rescued from their immorality by their participation in what was perceived to be a universal spirituality that was, in fact, a particular cultural-ecclesial spirituality and way of life."[2]

Albert J. Raboteau has explained:

"...black Catholics knew all too painfully that race did matter in the church in America. Though they might praise the church's universality in one breath, they actively protested discrimination with the next. The experience of black Catholics in the United States, then, has been an experience of alternating tension between the pull of universalism and the demands of racial particularism."[3]

The preceding scholars' astute observations outline a climate of obdurate cultural exclusion toward black Catholics within the mainstream American Roman Catholic Church. Nevertheless, functioning within this inhospitable context, black Catholics have consistently articulated their concerns about the institutional American Church's attitudes and policies toward them. This essay examines the thoughts a sampling of black Catholics expressed in petitions, correspondence, essays, and reviews which they wrote between 1817 and the 1940s, to demonstrate the deep historic roots of black Catholic consciousness of the frequently dialectical relationship they have experienced with their Church.

The first two examples date from the antebellum period and document the "righteous discontent" black Catholics felt who lacked access to Catholic education for their children. In 1817 six black signatories presented a Petition from the Catholic People of Color Residing in Philadelphia to a meeting of the Board of

---

[2] Jamie Phelps, OP, "Black Spirituality," in *Spiritual Traditions for the Contemporary Church* (Nashville: Abingdon Press, 1990), 346 cited in Thaddeus Posey, OFM Cap, "An Unwanted Commitment :The Spirituality of the Early Oblate Sisters of Providence, 1829-1990" (Ph. D. diss., Saint Louis University, 1993), 176.

[3] Albert J. Raboteau, *A Fire in the Bones: Reflections on African-American Religious History* (Boston: Beacon Press, 1995), 136.

Trustees of St. Mary's Church in that city. Identifying themselves as destitute but determined to resist the encouragement of the "different Sectarians" to send their children to Protestant schools, the men pleaded:

> "We tremble for the fate of our children, some of whom have already been seduced from our religion. Therefore we sincerely hope that your charitable board will take them under your protective wing as you have the poor of your own color and to have ours also instructed in a common English education [and catechism and prayers]."[4]

The Board ultimately took no action on this petition.

In 1853, Harriet Thompson, a black Catholic woman living in New York City, wrote a personal letter to the reigning Pontiff, Pope Pius IX. Concern "for the salvation of the black race in the United States who is going astray from neglect on the part of those who have care of souls" prompted Thompson to write her letter, shortly before the anticipated visit of the papal representative to the United States. Disclaiming any disrespect of clergy, "for which I would deserve punishment From god [sic] and From your Holiness," she nevertheless asserted that most bishops and clergy in the United States were ethnic Irish or Irish descent, "and not being accustom [sic] to the black race in Ireland, they can't think enough of them to take charge of their souls." Thompson continued, "Hence it is a great misstake [sic] to say that the church watches with equal care over every race and color, for how can it be said they teach all nations when they will not let the Black race mixt [sic] with the white...?"[5]

Thompson objected that black Catholics in the archdiocese of New York had no access to a Catholic education to counter the

---

[4] M. I. J. Griffin, "Petition of the Catholic People of Color in Philadelphia, 1817," in *American Catholic Historical Researches* VII (Philadelphia, 1890), 186.
[5] Harriet Thompson to Pope Pius IX, 29 October 1853, MPRF, Congressi: America Centrale, vol. 16, fols. 770 rv, 771 rv, 773 rv, 774 rv, 775 r, University of Notre Dame Archives.

influence of the blatant anti-Catholic bias of public school education. She contended that "the Catholics teach the pure word of god [sic] and gave learning at the same time; the Protestants gave learning and teach the word of god adulterated." Thompson then exposed the racist double standard of education operative in the archdiocese of New York. She asserted that "the church does remedy these evils for the white children by providing schools where they can learn the pure word of god and how to keep it and be educated at the same time, but the church do [sic] leave the colored children a prey to the wolf."[6]

Thompson recalled that in protest, "we the colored people of the cathedral congregation of the city of new york [sic]" had approached John Loughlin, Vicar-General of the archdiocese of New York, in 1849 to establish a school for black Catholic children. Racial consciousness and a strong Catholic identity, which had galvanized the Philadelphia petitioners to action previously, also motivated the black members of the Cathedral congregation of New York to mobilize and petition Loughlin. Although sympathetic to their cause, Loughlin lacked the authority to require the Sisters of Charity to integrate their schools, because Archbishop Hughes had refused to endorse the plan. Harriet Thompson understood that:

> "in new york nothing cannot [sic] be done because the Most Rev. Archbishop Hughes does not recognize the Black race to be a part of his flock...moreover it is well known by both white and black that the Most Reverend Archbishop Hughes do [sic] hate the black Race so much that he cannot bear them to come near him."

She further observed of Hughes's attitude, "this is very Hurtful indeed to think that the greatest Light the church has in America should dislike any creature Because it is the will of god that we should be of a darke Hue [sic]." Thompson appealed

---

[6] Ibid.

directly to the Pope to intercede: "I only write to pray your Holiness to take charge of our souls in your Holy Authority."[7]

Occasional misspellings and peculiarities of grammar and capitalization notwithstanding, Harriet Thompson's letter proved the work of a knowledgeable and perceptive community-oriented activist. She sought from Pope Pius IX a just resolution of the ecclesially-sanctioned racial discrimination confronting "the colored Catholics in most of the United States."[8] As if to verify that her personal voice represented more than an individual position, Thompson submitted to the pontiff the names of the seven married couples and thirteen individuals--eleven of them women--who had signed the petition to Rev. Loughlin.

Politically astute, Thompson further emphasized the critical condition of New York City's black Catholics by raising the spectre to the pope of "many Familis [sic] with the parents Catholics and the children protestants - overwhelmed with the belief that the name of Catholic amongst the black race will in a few years pass away." She also provided examples of the protestant "word of God adulterated" inculcated in black Catholic children in public schools: "the BLESSED EUCHARIST is nothing but a wafer; that the priest drinks the wine Himself [sic] and gives the bread to us; and that the Divine institution of confession is only to make money; and that the Roman Pontiff is Antichrist." Vatican authorities submitted Thompson's letter to the pope with the note "will be kept in mind when writing to American bishops."[9] Harriet Thompson's singular act in 1853 epitomized the exercise of black female Catholic agency in the antebellum United States.

After the abolition of slavery in 1865, the American Catholic hierarchy reluctantly addressed the prospect of four million freedmen as a vast mission field. Refusing to devote their own

---

[7] Ibid.
[8] Ibid.
[9] Ibid.

resources and manpower to this herculean task, the American clergy delegated this responsibility instead to the English St. Joseph's Society of the Sacred Heart, Mill Hill, a fledgling missionary band formed under the direction of Rev. Herbert Vaughan in 1871. The Josephites had vowed to serve black people exclusively in their American missions and Vaughan enjoined his priests strictly not to minister to white people. A series of letters black Catholics wrote to Vaughan between 1872 and 1878 document not only their assertions of themselves as American citizens and Roman Catholics, but also their keen awareness of the feelings of racial difference--if not revulsion--which plagued some of the English missionaries. In 1872 Rev. Vaughan embarked on a tour of New York City Roman Catholic churches to promote the Mill Hill Mission to the Colored and to solicit funds. Flyers announcing his visit exhorted the white public, "But after all, the present appeal is for the education of priests, whose lives will be spent in America; it is for a foreign race at your very doors--For the 5,000,000 Africans who will never become good Catholics and industrious citizens without your cooperation." New Yorker Charles L. Reason earned distinction as an educator, abolitionist, and political activist. In his letter to Vaughan, Reason identified himself as "a colored citizen and an attendant at St. Peter's," where Vaughan was to lecture, before stating his objections to the flyer language referring to the freedmen as a foreign race and as Africans. Reason explained:

> "Of all the inhabitants in that section of our country, they are the very native of the natives. Generation after generation for the last 250 years, have been born on the once slave plantations of the South....To plead for them, then, on the ground that they are a foreign race, is, it seems to me, not only violating facts, but it is a consenting to a weakening of what otherwise would be a powerful argument.--To me the whole strength of any appeal for the colored people of the South lies mainly in the truth that they are natives...and to represent them as a foreign race, Africans...is to foster a prejudice against them...whose malignity they have felt in no more bitter manner than from those who, coming from foreign lands, have found

these despised people objects on whom they could vent their spite, - naturalization turning these latter into Americans, while slavery and untold suffering only kept the others 'Africans'."[10]

The absurdity of *bona fide* foreign priests ministering to imputed "foreign" freedmen marginalized by race in America, undoubtedly did not escape Reason. His apt reference to the syndrome of European immigrants internalizing racism as part of their Americanization identified a malignancy which ensnared even some of the Mill Hill missionaries, as the following letters from black Catholic parishioners of St. Francis Xavier Church in Baltimore, Maryland, revealed.

After gratefully acknowledging the successful conversions the missionaries had accomplished in an 1873 letter to now Bishop Vaughan, an anonymous church member revealed:

> "Yet, my Lord, for the past three or four months there has been considerable dissatisfaction among the leading members of the Church. They feel as though our present Rector [Noonan] is not in sympathy with them, he like many foreigners who come to this country is fast imbibing the American prejudice against our race and has grown above the position he now occupies. It appears as though he has become disgusted with both Church and people. We pray you, most Noble Lord, to change our Rector and give us one... who is keenly alive to the interest of our people, one who is ever ready and always willing to do and suffer with us and is not ashamed to be identified with the Colored people or to be called their Priest...."

Noting that during the previous rectorship of

> "our lamented and beloved Fr. Dowling, on all occasions of business pertaining to the Church the most intelligent male members were called together and consulted as to the

---

[10] Charles L. Reason to Fr. Herbert Vaughan, 7 April 1872, 3 Mill Hill Transcripts 13 [hereinafter MHT], Josephite Fathers Archives, Maryland, [hereinafter JFA].

best method of raising and expending money to meet the current expenses of the Church. Now...no one is consulted or asked any questions concerning the Church affairs and no one knows what is to be done until it is over. If there is a dissatisfaction, we have to bear it in silence...."[11]

Black indignation at the white missionaries' palpable disrespect toward and thwarting of agency in their black parishioners resonated in other correspondence to Vaughan.

In 1875 Rector Noonan's reassignment of the universally loved Fr. James Gore to Charleston engendered significant dismay within St. Francis Xavier's congregation and prompted two letters to Vaughan from female parishioners. Although minimally literate, these women managed to convey their thoughts most effectively. Celestia Cook characterized "the lose of our holy Father Gore" as "a Cross that we can no longer stand and without your help we must fall in dispare...." Speaking "in behalf of all his distress Children and Converts wich are Coming into the fould onder Our dear Farther Gore instrouctin [*sic*], Cook feared "three third of the Congregasion will leave the Church" and "our Beutifull Sodality will be broke of." Cook's letter proves a study in contrasts. At times she employed the reverential tones of the supplicant in pleading, "holy father have mercy on his Poor Convert" or "O holy Bishop have mercy on your Poor Children [who] call epaint you for mercy as the thief Call Jesus when he hung on the Cross." At times she assumed the reproving tone of a challenger warning, "O Bishop dont you remember the Promise that you made us in the Pasts that our Priest should never be Sepparated from us untill death Sepparated us and if this is to be the case how can we place Confordence any more?"[12] This duality of supplicant and challenger Cook assumed in her letter characterized the approach Black Catholics would continue to use in their quest for inclusion in their Church for at least a century.

---

[11] An Anonymous Church Member to Bishop Vaughan, 6 July 1873, 4 MHT 24, JFA.
[12] Celestia Cook to Bishop Herbert Vaughan, 25 November 1875, 8 MHT 21, JFA.

The second anonymous female correspondent confirmed the congregation's deep affection for Fr. Gore and elaborated upon their dissatisfaction with Rector Noonan. She stated, "Father Gorr is bin tru to ous and never brokin his vouw since he has been hear he has saft a maney Soll from being lost for he goss in alles and plasis wher Father Nunnen said he would not go for when he coms out he has to have the Grippers taken of er him for the sak of saving poor Solls from being lost." She further revealed the role ethnic antipathies played in their dissatisfaction, saying of the Irish, "In tim of the Mishin we could hardly get in our Puy for the Parish. Father Nunnen hear thear Confashen so thay thing they have the best insight of the schursh is to good fore Niggros." She continued, "Father Nunnen dont take intrust in us as Father Gorr and other Preast as Father Nunnen came hear for ous our deiechtor and the Irrish is trying to taing him from ous. In stet we rutting them out they ar rutting ous out. Father Nunen invited them to come [*sic*]." Finally, this author revealed a judicious blend of the spiritual and the practical in her problem solving method. She acknowledged, "We are all praying very hard but by a few words you Say will do more good than praying, alldo we will never rest to pray...."[13] As these two letters demonstrate, supplication, challenge, and practicality remained proven weapons in the black Catholic arsenal.

The urgent pleas of James Gore's devoted black parishioners did not prevent Rector Noonan from reassigning him to Charleston. However, Noonan himself corroborated the validity of his black congregation's articulated grievances against him. In his own correspondence with Bishop Vaughan between 1872 and 1877, Noonan confessed to, "the repugnance which I first felt on coming among the blacks."[14] His Josephite colleagues concurred in Fr. Gore's assessment that Noonan "has no vocation for the

---

[13] A Negro (Negress) to Bishop Herbert Vaughan, 26 November 1875, 8 MHT 22, JFA.
[14] James Noonan to Bishop Herbert Vaughan, 24 April 1873, 4 MHT 13b; 23 June 1873, 4 MHT 23a, JFA.

colored people...it is with great difficulty that he can speak a <u>kind</u> word to these poor outcast down-trodden people - Many a time my heart has bled at the harsh rough unkind way in which he has treated them - he does not <u>cannot</u> love them...[emphasis his]"[15] In 1877 James Noonan left the Josephite Society.

Successful resolution of the problems presented in the preceding petitions and correspondence proves less historically significant than the fact that positive senses of themselves as black people and their fervent internalization of and adherence to Roman Catholicism both impelled and empowered such nineteenth-century black Roman Catholics-- whether female or male, well-educated or barely literate, impoverished or prosperous, northern or southern--to inform Church authorities of their concerns and to expect redress of their problems.

Two examples of individual black Catholic protest from the twentieth century conclude this essay. In her doctoral dissertation, "A Brilliant Possibility: The Cardinal Gibbons Institute, 1924-1934," Dr. Cecilia Moore describes the influence of the indomitable Constance E. H. Daniel. Daniel, a graduate of Atlanta University, converted to Roman Catholicism after marrying her husband, Victor Daniel,)in 1916. From 1924 until 1934, he served as the principal; she, the assistant principal and matron of the Cardinal Gibbons Institute (CGI) in Ridge, Maryland. Conceived as an experiment in Catholic vocational education for black people, the Institute proved a battleground for control between black and white constituencies as well as conflicting theories of education.

Constance Daniel never minced words. She once boldly observed to Archbishop Michael Curley of Baltimore, "You and I understand each other very well. You are very imperious and I am very tenacious."[16] A white male opponent to Daniel on the CGI

---

[15] James Gore to Bishop Herbert Vaughan, 22 June, 1873, 4 MHT 21, JFA.
[16] Constance Daniel to Archbishop Michael Curley, 14 April 1934, Curley Correspondence, D144, Archives of the Archdiocese of Baltimore, cited in

Board confided to the archbishop, "he [Daniel] is governed almost entirely by his wife, who is a very strong character, and who, I fear, has the idea that the Negro is not only as good as the White man, but a little better...."[17]

In 1930 Constance Daniel reviewed Rev. John T. Gillard's controversial book, *The Catholic Church and the American Negro*, in the Urban League's organ, *Opportunity, A Journal of Negro Life*. She duly gave him "all credit for having made available much needed data on the Negro missions" and "making some very pertinent and sane comments on certain phases of Negro development." However, Daniel devotes most of the review to lambasting Gillard's "tactless blunderings of a young and over-zealous priest...unable apparently to see his subject without the aid of someone else's glasses--which happen to be out of focus." Gillard frequently incorporated racial stereotypes uncritically in his study. References to "the childlike mentality of this infantine race," and such assertions as "the high intellectual requirements of the priesthood immediately eliminate the majority of the race," or "There can be little room for doubt that his view of religion as an emotional experience only has had a detrimental effect upon the character of the Negro [so] that the emotions predominate at the expense of that clear, calm judgment so necessary for the proper evaluation of moral standards" fueled the fire of Daniel's indignation. She also excoriated Gillard for accepting current Catholic practices of racially segregated education from the primary levels through college--"in face of the fact that scores of Negro students matriculate yearly without difficulty at Northern and Mid-Western universities." Daniel concluded her scathing review presciently, "Some day when he has independently searched for the truth and made it his own, we hope that more

---

Cecilia A. Moore, "A Brilliant Possibility: The Cardinal Gibbons Institute, 1924 - 1934" (Ph. D. diss., University of Virginia, 1997), 297.

[17] Admiral William S. Benson to Archbishop Michael J. Curley, 17 October 1927, Curley Correspondence, B732, Archives of the Archdiocese of Baltimore, cited in Moore, "A Brilliant Possibility," 147.

consistent, more mature, and more courteous Father Gillard will write again."[18]

In 1941 Gillard wrote *Colored Catholics in the United States*. While still maintaining that "[t]he Southern attitude requires tact and patience...," Gillard now insisted that "[o]utside of States which have segregation laws, all parochial, high, college, and university educational facilities must be made available to Negroes if they are able to meet the same requirements as those demanded of white pupils."[19] His active involvement in the Catholic Students' Mission Crusade (CSMC) contributed substantively to the eventual integration of Catholic higher education.

In 1941 Lois Sherer, a young black Catholic alumna of and future lay teacher at St. Frances Academy, the historic institution under the direction of the Oblate Sisters of Providence in Baltimore, published an essay, "Let's Be Honest With the Negro," in *The Shield*,[20] the official organ of the CSMC. She had delivered this essay the previous June at the CSMC convention, at which Gillard had delivered the keynote address. The piece definitely reflected Sherer's own thoughts and experiences, but Gillard had clearly edited the essay. In being Gillard's protégé, Sherer also became his avatar, giving voice to some of his thoughts interpolated through a black, female persona. Perhaps Gillard had complied partially with Daniel's stipulation that "he independently search for the truth and make it his own."

The essay began with the statement, "I am a Negro. I do not think it necessary to apologize because I am a Negro." She

---

[18] Constance E. H. Daniel, review of *The Catholic Church and the American Negro* by Rev. John T. Gillard, SSJ, in *Opportunity: A Journal of Negro Life* (August, 1930): 247-48; internal citations from John T. Gillard, SSJ, *The Catholic Church and the American Negro* (Baltimore: St. Joseph Society Press, 1929), 82, 88, 244.

[19] John T. Gillard, *Colored Catholics in the United States*, (Baltimore: The Josephite Press, 1941), 244, 260.

[20] Lois Sherer, "Let's Be Honest with the Negro," in *The Shield*, October 1940: 9-10, in John T. Gillard Papers, F 50 A, Box 2, JFA.

defended Negro history and culture as sources of pride, "even though my forebears did not go so far in culture as did yours" and declared herself an American because of the horrors of enslavement and the contributions of the enslaved to the building of the American nation. As if to reassure a skittish white audience--perhaps at Gillard's insistence--Sherer included the following enigmatic passage:

> "But this is all history. I am willing to forget it. I am proud to be an American because in spite of the fact that as a Negro I may not be entirely free in this land of the free, I can be brave in this land of the brave. I am proud to be an American because, in spite of the fact that I am deprived of the exercise of many of the rights guaranteed by the Constitution, I still have those rights and can hope for their full attainment."

Sherer continued, "I am a Catholic" and explained that Fr. Gillard had baptized her, her mother, and sister eight years before.

> "Father Gillard taught me that the Catholic Church wants all the Negroes, that the Catholic Church welcomes all races and all peoples, and that the Negro Catholic is as much a Catholic as any Catholic in the world. I believe all these things that Father taught me because I know that the Catholic Church, being the true Church cannot be wrong. But I am not so sure that some Catholics are so sincere as their Church...I have been a Catholic for eight years, yet in all that time I have never had the courage to venture into a white Catholic Church, because I was afraid that I would not be welcome.

> "Take the matter of Catholic schools. I have Catholic friends who must go to public schools simply because the Catholic schools will not take colored pupils, although they welcome Protestants and Jews. I am fortunate in having had a Catholic high school education and in being enrolled already in a Catholic college for the fall opening; but how many colored Catholics there are who are denied these blessings just because they are colored.

> "Now, let's be honest with the Negro. Do you want us in the Catholic Church or don't you? Is your love of the Blessed Sacrament strong enough not to faint if you have to hear Mass sitting in a pew with a Negro Catholic?...Is your love for souls sincere enough to sit in a classroom with a Negro as well as with a Protestant or a Jew? Let's be honest with the Negro, or rather let's be honest with Christ....I would make a distinction between the Catholic Church and Catholics. I would say that the Catholic Church is the greatest Church in the world because it is the only true Church in the world. But white Catholics--some of them have frightened me to death."[21]

Significantly, Sherer's challenge to white Catholics reiterated all the themes black Catholics had expressed over time in the documents examined in this essay: explicit self-identification as black people, Roman Catholics, and Americans; access to Catholic education; respect of black personhood, history, and culture from white Catholics; and greater inclusion of people of color in the Mystical Body of Christ.

As contemporary scholar Albert Raboteau has perceptively observed, "Unless we recognize cultural particularism, universalism becomes another word for the cultural hegemony of the dominant group. Black Catholic history reaffirms an old truth: the Church must never be confused with any particular ethnic group, race, culture, or period. The Church does indeed transcend race, but only by including all races within its embrace, as equally valuable children, whose differences and unique contributions help us to build up the body of Christ."[22]

---

[21] Ibid.
[22] Raboteau, *A Fire in the Bones*, 137.

WORKS CITED

Primary Sources:

John T. Gillard Papers, Josephite Fathers Archives, Baltimore, Maryland.

Mill Hill Transcripts, Josephite Fathers Archives, Baltimore, Maryland.

Propaganda Fide Archives Microfilm, University of Notre Dame Archives, South Bend, Indiana.

Secondary Sources:

Daniel, Constance E.H. Review of *The Catholic Church and the American Negro* by Rev. John T. Gillard, S.S.J. In *Opportunity: A Journal of Negro Life* (August 1930): 247-48.

Davis, Cyprian, O.S.B. *The History of Black Catholics in the United States*. New York:Crossroad, 1990.

Gillard, John T., S.S.J. *The Catholic Church and the American Negro*. Baltimore: St. Joseph Society Press, 1929.

_____. *Colored Catholics in the United States*. Baltimore: The Josephite Press, 1941.

Griffin, M. I. J. "Petition of the Catholic People of Color in Philadelphia, 1817." *American Catholic Historical Researches* VII (1890): 186.

Moore, Cecilia A. "A Brilliant Possibility: The Cardinal Gibbons Institute, 1924-1934." Ph.D. diss., University of Virginia, 1997.

Posey, Thaddeus J., O.F.M., Cap. "An Unwanted Commitment: The Spirituality of the Early Oblate Sisters of Providence, 1829-1890." Ph.D. diss., St. Louis University. 1993.

Raboteau, Albert J. *A Fire in the Bones: Reflections on African American Religious History.* Boston: Beacon Press, 1995.

Sherer, Lois. "Let's be Honest With the Negro." *The Shield* (October 1940): 9-10, in the John T. Gillard Papers, Josephite Fathers Archives, Baltimore, Maryland.

Redemptive Suffering and Christology in African American Christian Theology

Nathaniel Holmes, Jr.
Florida Memorial University, Miami

In this paper, based on a presentation delivered at the 2009 Annual Meeting at the Atlanta University Center, Holmes engages the debate over the redemptive nature of suffering in Christianity. Are evil, suffering, and oppression redemptive, thereby bringing us closer to the divine? Or, are suffering and oppression detrimental to the salvific nature of Christ's liberation? Holmes explores the religious and philosophical literary tradition of redemptive suffering, especially as interpreted in African American religious thought, and shows us that the answers to these questions are complex and multifaceted.

Over the past few decades, *suffering* has become the *de facto* litmus test for theological engagement.[1] Human experience is a fundamental source of theology, and theologians from all walks of life have sought to relate the Christian tradition to struggles of liberation, equality, and social and environmental justice. The language of suffering is used frequently in religion and politics.[2] Suffering, as terminology, has no functional or operational quality apart from religious, theological, and philosophical frameworks. Thus, any adequate understanding of suffering must include its religious and theological dimensions. Theologians have always struggled with the complex cluster of questions and queries regarding the meaning and value of life in light of issues such as the problem of evil, misery and suffering. One aspect of theodicy that is prevalent (and for some problematic) in Christianity is that

---

[1] Arthur C. McGill, *Suffering: A Test of Theological Method* (Philadelphia, PA: The Westminster Press, 2007), p. 7.
[2] See for example, Peter Dews, *The Idea of Evil* (Malden, MA: Blackwell Publishing, 2007), pp. 1-17.

evil and suffering are redeemable, or evil and suffering serve a divine purpose.

Some theologians (e.g., Delores Williams, Anthony Pinn) reject the idea that suffering can be redeemable in any possible way. I believe, however, that this leads to a christological problem. If we reject the principle of redemptive suffering, how do we interpret the death of Jesus the Christ? How can we both affirm with the Christian tradition that Christ's death was to redeem humanity from sin, while at the same time deny that any suffering is redemptive? The African American Christian theological tradition is an excellent theological apparatus to reflect on the notion of redemptive suffering. African American religious thought is essentially a response to the atrocities Black people have faced because of our subjugation, enslavement, and dehumanization.[3] Redemptive suffering has a long and deep history in African American theology.

The purpose of this paper is to reappraise the notion of redemptive suffering, in light of a central Christian symbol, i.e., the suffering of Jesus Christ as achieving a divine aim/goal, within African American Christian theology. After outlining some of the salient theological and sociological positions both for and against redemptive suffering, and indicating the chief biblical texts employed to substantiate each position, I will show how christological potholes have been created and/or glossed over by both those who support and those who outright reject redemptive suffering. On the one hand, Christ stands against all forms of oppression and suffering, demonstrated as he tried to alleviate suffering through his ministry (via healing, providing food, etc).[4] At the same time, though, Christ constantly maintained that his own suffering was an essential element of divine means for human

---

[3] Charles Long, "Perspectives for a Study of African American Religion in the United States" in Larry G. Murphy, ed., *Down By the Riverside: Readings in African American Religion* (New York, NY: New York University Press, 2000), pp. 10-11.
[4] James Cone, *A Black Theology of Liberation* (Maryknoll, NY: Orbis Books, 1971), p. 116.

salvation. In light of the salvific character of christological witness, can we normatively say that there is *no* value in suffering? Or are all claims of redemptive suffering detrimental to any theology of liberation and re-humanization? I hope to do two things: 1) reopen provocative and critical discussion about how we define and employ "suffering" in theology (and politics), particularly with regard to redemptive suffering; and 2) show that blanket statements for or against redemptive suffering are largely inadequate and erroneous.

The Problem of Evil in Christian Thought

Questions regarding the meaning and value of life in light of evil, misery and suffering, are long-standing, especially as it relates to religious beliefs.[5] The religious problem of evil arises from the seeming contradiction in affirming both the existence of an omnipotent, omnibenevolent God along with the existence of evil and suffering in the world.[6] David Hume argued that the existence of evil in the world is inconsistent with the existence of God.[7] Evil and suffering, Hume maintained, presents compelling evidence against the existence of God. Theodicy is the attempt to validate the goodness, power, and/or providential care of God in the face of horrendous evils. Generally, theologians and philosophers have distinguished between two types of evil: moral and natural. Moral evil comprises all "bad" things for which human beings are morally responsible. Natural evil signifies the events that occur "in nature" of their own accord that cause devastation for human beings, such as, hurricanes or diseases.

---

[5] Michael L. Peterson, "The Problem of Evil" in Phillip L. Quinn and Charles Taliaferro, *A Companion to Philosophy of Religion* (Oxford, UK: Blackwell Publishing Ltd, 1997), p. 393.
[6] Epicurus expresses the problem of evil succinctly when he says "Is he (God) willing to prevent evil, but not able? Then he is impotent. Is he able, but not willing? Then he is malevolent. Is he both able and willing? Whence then is evil?"
[7] David Hume, *Dialogues Concerning Natural Religion 2nd Edition, Edited with an Introduction by Richard H. Popkin* (Hackett Publishing Company Inc, 1998), pp. 58-76.

A prevalent notion in some Christian theologies is all evil and suffering in the world exists because of the "fall" of humanity. In fact, for some thinkers "to speak of human redemption necessarily presupposes the fall of [humanity]."[8] Adam and Eve transgressed the divine command given in the Garden of Eden, fell from the "state of innocence" in which God created them, and through them, the entire human race has been affected by this transgression. The position that posits human sin as the source of evil and suffering is called the free-will defense and it tries to show that it is logically possible that an all-powerful and all good God is responsible for the existence of this world and that all evil may ultimately result from misuse of creaturely freedom. This standpoint is grounded in the Augustinian notion of a "Fall" from grace by free, perfect finite creatures – angels and human beings – that affected the physical world as well. For Augustine, God created Adam (and more pointedly Adam's soul) in God's own image and placed in him the souls of all human beings that were going to exist. God created Adam in righteousness and in freedom and because of the misuse of this freedom the image of God in Adam –and subsequently, in all humans –was distorted. "[The] man was willingly perverted and justly condemned, and so begot perverted and condemned offspring...man could not be born of man in any other condition. Hence from the misuse of free will there started a chain of disasters."[9] The chain of disasters included the natural world. A problem that is inherent in Augustine's theodicy is that evil is self-created "ex nihilo."

Modern treatment of the free-will defense can be seen in the work of Stephen Davis. He argues that the attempts to portray the notions of an all-powerful, all loving God and the existence of evil as being logically inconsistent are false. He rejects any solutions to the theodicy issue that deny the existence of evil, the perfect goodness of God, or God's omnipotence. Davis distinguishes

---

[8] James Theodore Holly, "The Divine Plan of Human Redemption" in Anthony Pinn, *Moral Evil and Redemptive Suffering: A History of Theodicy in African American Religious Thought* (Gainesville, FL: University of Florida Press, 2002), p. 133
[9] Augustine, *City of God*, Book 13, Chapter 14.

between two aspects to the problem of evil: the logical problem of evil (LPE) and the emotive problem of evil (EPE). The logical problem strives to show that God's omnipotence, God's omnibenevolence, and the existence of evil exists are logically consistent. According to the free-will defense God had two main aims. First, God wanted to create the best universe possible, i.e., the best possible balance of moral and natural good over moral and natural evil. Second, God wanted to create a world in which rational beings freely choose to love and obey God.[10] The quandary with God creating human beings in freedom is that the possibility for doing evil is unavoidably incorporated. Davis acknowledges that God is indirectly responsible for evil in that God created the circumstances by which evil could come into being. However, the existence of evil was not necessary. Humans chose to disobey God and the result was sin and evil. God is vindicated because this is the best possible world that could be created with free moral agents.

For John Hick the theodicy "project" is an exercise in metaphysical thinking, in the sense that it consists in the development and analysis of all-encompassing hypotheses concerning the nature and process of the universe. There are two criteria that a theodicy has to meet: 1) it must be internally coherent and 2) it must be consistent with the data both of the religious tradition on which it is based, and of the world, i.e., evidence revealed by scientific excavation and specific facts about moral and natural evil.[11] Hick argues from the Irenaean tradition instead of the Augustinian tradition.[12] Irenaeus did not develop a theodicy himself, but he did, according to Hick, provide a framework for a theodicy that does contain the idea of a "Fall" and is consistent with modern scientific theory concerning the origins of the human race. Irenaeus distinguished between the image of God and the likeness of God in humanity. The "image" resides in

---

[10] Stephen Davis, "Free Will and Evil", in Stephen Davis, ed., *Encountering Evil* (Louisville, KY: Westminster John Knox Press, 2001), p. 74.
[11] John Hick, "An Irenaean Theodicy", in Stephen Davis, *Encountering Evil*, p. 38.
[12] Ibid, p. 39.

a human's bodily form and represents one's nature as an intelligent being capable of fellowship with God. The "likeness" represents the perfecting of human beings by the Holy Spirit. Irenaeus believed that human beings were created as immature entities that needed to grow until they became perfectly like the creator.[13]

The fundamental theme of the Irenaean theodicy is divided into two-stage conception. The first stage was "the gradual production of homo sapiens, through the long evolutionary process, as intelligent ethical and religious animals."[14] This perception of early humanity does not include the Augustinian vision of a harmonious period between humans and God. Instead, life of early humanity was filled with exertion against a hostile environment, necessitating the capacity for savage violence against fellow human beings, especially outside of one's immediate community. [15] Humanity was created only with the *potential* for knowledge of and relationship with the creator. Because of this the second stage consists of the intelligent, ethical, and religious animals being brought through their own free consciousness into what Irenaeus called the divine likeness. An important factor of the second stage is that humanity participates in this process.

Irenaean theodicy argues that human beings were created imperfectly for a divine purpose, namely, so that human freedom could be fully actualized. "For what freedom could finite beings have in an immediate consciousness of the one who has created them, who knows them through and through, who is limitlessly powerful as well as limitlessly loving and good, and who claims their total obedience?"[16] Furthermore, the premise that God created human beings at an epistemic distance from God's self in order that we may gradually achieve the likeness of God through

---

[13] John Hick, *Evil and the God of Love*, (San Francisco, CA: Harper and Row Publishers, 1978), pp. 211-212.
[14] Hick, "An Irenaean Theodicy", p. 40.
[15] Ibid.
[16] Ibid, p. 42.

our own moral and spiritual faculties, necessitates that the physical environment (the world) to be one that is filled with challenges, pain, dangers, as well as, success, happiness, and progress.[17]

The divine intention in relation to humanity is to create perfect finite human beings in filial relationship with their creator. It is not logically possible for human beings to already be created in this perfect state because, from a spiritual aspect, a perfect finite being includes coming freely to an uncoerced consciousness of God from a situation of epistemic distance, and in a moral aspect, freely choosing the good. Human beings were created through the evolutionary process, as spiritually and morally immature creature, as part of a religiously ambiguous and ethically demanding world. Therefore, moral and natural evil are necessary aspects of the present stage of the process through which God is gradually creating perfect finite human beings.

I see Irenaean theodicy as a foundation for redemptive suffering. Moral and natural evil exist for a divine teleological aim for human existence, namely that humans become perfect finite creatures. Suffering, then, is instructive and edifying. Indeed, human beings can only achieve union with the divine through evil and suffering.

Redemptive Suffering

> *"As he walked along, he saw a man blind from birth. His disciples asked him, 'Rabbi, who sinned, this man or his parents, that he was born blind?' Jesus answered, 'Neither this man nor his parents, that he was born blind so that God's works might be revealed in him."*[18]

An aspect of theodicy that is prevalent and problematic in Christianity is that evil and suffering are redeemable, or evil and suffering serve a divine purpose. In some theological traditions,

---

[17] Ibid, p. 47.
[18] John 9:1-3 in *The New Oxford Annotated Bible, New Revised Standard Version, 3rd Edition* (New York, NY: Oxford university Press, Inc, 2001).

redemptive suffering is the belief that human suffering, when offered with the sufferings of Jesus, can remit the just punishment of one's sins or those of another.[19] Still others appeal to the notion that unmerited suffering will be compensated through some heavenly reward to be received in the Day of Judgment.[20] In this essay, redemptive suffering is the idea that suffering is employed for a divine purpose or aim, i.e., God creates or permits instances, situations, of suffering with the intent of securing some greater good.[21]

Christian understandings of evil and suffering stem from first century Jewish religious thought. Response to evil and suffering in first century B.C.E. Judaism was connected to the ways in which Jews perceived the significance of the coming of the Messiah.[22] The coming of the Messiah was God's assurance that Israel had not been abandoned to a world of injustice and affliction. In essence, Christ (Messiah) was the solution to the problems of evil and suffering. It is the Christ who eventually brings an end to suffering and evil when he ushers in the new eschaton.[23] The focus, though, is towards the future. We anticipate the time when the eradication of evil and suffering will occur. Therefore, we must tolerate suffering in the present. This line of thinking influences the Christian tradition. In keeping with the Jewish tradition of his day, the Apostle Paul viewed suffering as something we must "endure for the present, with the hope that relief would be provided by the coming eschaton."[24]

---

[19] See Richard P. McBrien, *Catholicism: New Study Edition* (New York, NY: HarperCollins Publishers, 1994), pp. 345-346.
[20] Leslie Montgomery, *Redemptive Suffering: Lessons Learned from the Garden of Gethsemane* (Wheaton, IL: Crossway Books, 2006), p. 35.
[21] Anthony Pinn, *Why Lord? Suffering and Evil in Black Theology* (New York, NY: Continuum Press, 1995), p. 15.
[22] Telford Work, "Advent's Answer to the Problem of Evil" in *International Journal of Systematic Theology* 2, no. 1 (March 2000): 100-111.
[23] John Swinton, *Raging With Compassion: Pastoral Responses to the Problem of Evil* (Grand Rapids, MI: William B. Eerdmans Publishing Company, 2007), p. 37.
[24] Ibid.

Again, we see seeds of redemptive suffering. It is not simply the fact that suffering is a current and pervasive reality; rather it is the attitude that one *must endure* suffering until some future eschaton. Over time, the tradition developed rewards and incentives for those who are able to endure faithfully, supported with the belief that suffering is for a purpose.[25] Characterizations of redemptive suffering tend to fall into two general categories: 1) suffering is redemptive because it is pedagogical in nature (i.e., human beings learn, experience transformation, and gain wisdom through suffering), and 2) suffering is redemptive because it is punitive in nature (i.e., suffering is deserved punishment for sin).[26] Each of these categories operates with the assumption that suffering is to be endured and it is for divine purposes (regardless of our capacity to discern what these purposes may be).

Redemptive suffering has been given philosophical justifications as well. Leibniz, for example, argued that the world (with all its instances of evil and suffering) could not have been created better than it has been.[27] This would be to deny the complete omnibenevolence of God. Consequently, Leibniz said, the causal connections between moral and physical evils that are unknown would be explicated with the progress of science. Thus, we would eventually discover that suffering is ultimately the effect of human sin. We would also determine that suffering itself is the "cause of some greater good."[28]

---

[25] This is reinforced by a doctrine of God that views God as in complete control of the happenings of the world. Classical Christian orthodoxy adopted the Greek metaphysical models of God. Among them is the perfection of God. Perfection includes categories such as omnipotence. The traditional understanding of omnipotence has been a problem for theodicy because it suggests that God determines and controls all events that occur, including evil. It also implies that God is unwilling to alleviate suffering and eradicate evil instantaneously.
[26] Anthony Pinn, *Moral Evil and Redemptive Suffering*, p. 8.
[27] See Gottfried Wilhelm Leibniz, *Theodicy* Edited by Austin Farrar, Trans. by E. M. Huggard (BiblioBazaar, 2007).
[28] Susan Neiman, *Evil in Modern Thought: An Alternative History of Philosophy* (Princeton, NJ: Princeton University Press, 2002), p. 30.

More importantly, redemptive suffering is very much active in popular religious belief. The fundamental aim is to find, discern, or make *meaning* from the reality of suffering. As one person frames it, finding the "yes" in suffering is the work of redemptive suffering.[29] In other words, we must find strength in weakness, power in powerlessness, and life in death. Suffering becomes a mystery, an unexplainable reality that one must endure with faith intact.

Finally, for the present task, redemptive suffering finds its greatest power (in the Christian tradition) in the sufferings and death of Jesus Christ. Though the crucifixion of Christ is interpreted in various ways, one common theme is that Christ's sufferings were for the benefit of others and his death and resurrection defied the demonic forces of sin and oppression. James Mohler, for example, argues that suffering is holy to Christians because suffering is "sanctified" by the cross.[30] He goes as far as to claim Jesus himself is the sacrament of suffering.[31] Since the church is Christ's body we must also suffer. We are reminded that Christ commands his disciples to take up their crosses and follow his example.

Redemptive Suffering in African American Religious Thought

Redemptive Suffering is the dominant conceptualization concerning suffering among African Americans.[32] African Americans continue to affirm the iniquitous character of suffering (i.e., slavery, disenfranchisement, etc.) while maintaining that God can, and will, bring about a more beneficial and blessed situation for African Americans *through* their sufferings. The primary

---

[29] Juliana Cooper-Goldenburg, "Redemptive Suffering" at www.stripedrock.org/all_for_seniors/pdf/articles/RedemptiveSuffering.pdf

[30] James Aylward Mohler, *The Sacrament of Suffering: The Meeting of God and Man in Suffering Can Be A Way to Complete and Final Fulfillment* (Notre Dame, IN: Fides/Claretian, 1979), p. vii.

[31] Ibid.

[32] Anthony Pinn, *Moral Evil and Redemptive Suffering*, p. 8. See Also Quinton Dixie and Cornel West, *The Courage to Hope: From Black Suffering to Human Redemption* (Boston, MA: Beacon Press, 1999).

image that has persisted is that of God as a liberator. This image developed out of the condition of slavery as one of the buffers to dehumanization. Liberation means both freedom from this present life to an 'otherworldly" existence (heaven), and freedom from oppression and bondage.[33] During American slavery, enslavers preached that the condition of African-Americans was the will of God. The enslaved, on the other hand, rejected this claim, and opted for the belief that God's will was for them to be free.

In the theology of enslaved African Americans, Jesus as the Christ is the crucial manifestation of the divine presence that standardizes God's nature as liberator and savior. Jesus played an important role in the religion of the enslaved (not the religion that the enslavers wished the enslaved to adopt) because of his own contextual condition. Jesus was a Jew – a part of a nation of people that had been enslaved but God delivered, Jesus was a poor Jew, and he was a member of a minority group in the midst of a larger dominant controlling group (the Romans).[34] Basically, what African-American women and men in bondage saw in Jesus was someone who had lived under conditions of oppression, proclaimed the divine message of liberation in spite of oppression, was crucified by his oppressors, but gained victory over them through his resurrection and the power to liberate others who are in bondage.

Jesus was considered as a friend (the one who would never forsake you in trials and tribulation), converter in conversion, mother (the one nurtures and takes care of you), and the very incarnation of the divine purpose of human freedom. These characteristics of Jesus are significant in the religion of the enslaved because they repudiated the Christ preached by the dominant society encouraging them to be good, faithful, and

---

[33] J. Deotis Roberts, *Liberation and Reconciliation: A Black Theology* (Louisville, KY: Westminster John Knox Press, 2005), pp. 8-11. See also J. Deotis Roberts, *Black Religion, Black Theology: The Collected Essays of J. Deotis Roberts* (Harrisburg, PA: Trinity Press International, 2003), pp. 43-47.
[34] Howard Thurman, *Jesus & the Disinherited*, (Boston, MA: Beacon Press 1976), pp. 15-18.

honest – obeying their masters and accepting that their enslavement was divinely sanctioned. Nevertheless, the liberation from slavery would be gradual. The present condition of slavery was something that had to be endured. Entrenched in slave religion was the belief that God had plans for the enslaved beyond slavery, and that they "only had to wait on God, trust in God and persevere."[35]

David Walker saw the depiction of God as just and righteous and the continued subjugation of African Americans as mutually exclusive realities. For him, God was unequivocally against the brutal treatment of African Americans.[36] It is unthinkable that the enslavement and oppression of African Americans was divinely sanctioned since God is indeed kind, just, loving, and righteous.[37] Thus, God works towards the liberation of the enslaved and oppressed, and establishing justice and equality in society. In certain respects, however, Walker suggests that slavery was permitted for pedagogical reasons.[38] He asserted that while God is not the cause of slavery, there was value in slavery.

A strong "other-worldly" emphasis existed among the masses of Black America, particularly as expressed in African American literature from the mid-nineteenth to early twentieth century.[39] Historical evidence suggests that the mass of Black Americans did work for social equality, especially through support of their local churches and national church conventions. Yet, it is not surprising to see expressions of hope mainly in a world to come, rather than complete hope for a better world in this life. After all, there were no grandiose signs of the dominant white culture and society

---

[35] Anthony Pinn, *Why Lord? Suffering and Evil in Black Theology*, p. 29.
[36] See David Walker, *David Walker's Appeal: To the Coloured Citizens of the World* (Pennsylvania State University Press, 2002). For an exposition on the life and thought of David Walker see Rufus Burrow, *God and Human Responsibility: David Walker and Ethical Prophecy* (Macon, GA: Mercer University Press, 2004).
[37] Anthony Pinn, *Why Lord? Suffering and Evil in Black Theology*, p. 41.
[38] Ibid, pp. 42-43
[39] See Benjamin Mays, *The Negro's God*, (New York, NY: Atheneum Publishing, 1938).

repenting of its propagation of racial oppression and overwhelmingly eradicating the structures that kept African Americans in poverty, uneducated, etc. Hope had to be in God and in a world where equality and justice was assured.

The idea was that God would bring about complete liberation in God's own time. Everything will eventually work out, maybe in this world, but if not, then the next world. God was preparing a "home in glory" for those who were faithful in their lives despite the horrible afflictions of existence. For much of Black America it was futile to expect good from American society and hope of rectifying their situations themselves because they were powerless. Only God had the power and God's will was seemingly that Blacks suffer in this life to receive greater rewards in the next.

Earl Carter suggests the enslavement of Africans and African Americans was the will of God in order for them to encounter the gospel of Jesus Christ. This enslavement was also punishment for the idolatrous practices of ancient African civilizations (specifically Egypt and Ethiopia).[40] Carter predicates this upon the God's behavior with Israel as delineated in the Book of Judges and several other passages of Scripture. The point is that God is the source of African American enslavement (and by extension African American suffering).[41] European Americans were simply instruments of divine actions.[42] One can conjecture from Carter's claims that suffering can serve both as divine punishment for sin and idolatry (even if the punishment is upon a future generation for the transgressions of a past generation), as well as, a means to develop a deeper relationship between God and a group of people. In either case, evil and suffering serve a divine purpose.

According to Anthony Pinn, African-Americans have engaged in discourse concerning the problem of evil in a manner corresponding to three propositions, namely, rethinking the nature

---

[40] Earl Carter, *No Apology Necessary* (Creation House, 1997), pp. 35-41.
[41] Ibid, p. 115.
[42] Ibid.

of evil, rethinking the power of God, and rethinking God's goodness or righteousness. This is seen in Black theological thought suggesting that: 1) unmerited suffering is intrinsically evil, yet can have redemptive consequences, 2) God and humans are coworkers in the struggle to remove moral evil, or 3) Black suffering may result from God being a racist.[43] Position number one posits that suffering is a temporary evil known to and manipulated by God for the Christian's ultimate benefit. This is the notion of redemptive suffering. Unmerited existential adversity is evil, but it can have resulting remuneration. These rewards may entail correction of character flaws, obtainment of invaluable skills and talents, or a future reward from God in an afterlife. Basically, evil and suffering in this life serves a divine aim. Redemptive evil and suffering is purported because people wish to maintain the traditional religious symbols of God. Pinn argues that human liberation and life quality are more important than maintaining a religious symbol. Any theological symbol that does not coincide with a theodicy that takes evil and suffering seriously, as well as, provide a basis for countering evil and suffering in the world must be discarded.

Rejecting a religious symbol because of its (potential) oppressive connotations is a hallmark of strong humanism.[44] Pinn says that strong humanism offers a viable solution to the problem of evil because it does not privilege theological categories over the reality of suffering.[45] Theodicy, for example, can play no role in

---

[43] Anthony Pinn, *Why Lord? Suffering and Evil in Black Theology*, p. 15

[44] Pinn offers two types of humanism: weak humanism and strong humanism. Weak humanism questions the theological assertion of God's omnipotence. It concludes that God does not possess "all-power" and human beings should not rely solely on God's ability to eliminate suffering, evil, and oppression. We must work with God to bring achieve liberation. Strong humanism, however, questions the very existence of God and the validity of any theological propositions that are contradictory to the reality of the Black experience of suffering and the quest for Black liberation.

[45] Anthony Pinn, *Why Lord? Suffering and Evil in Black Theology*, p. 18. Pinn sees strong humanism as a religious system in itself as it provides a framework that guides human conduct and connects to a larger reality, particularly the reality of African Americans. He grounds this claim in the Clifford Geertz's definition of religion.

strong humanism because theodicy assumes the omnibenevolence of God and necessitates that we discern value in suffering.[46] Strong humanism unequivocally maintains that there are no redemptive qualities in suffering.[47] Although strong humanism questions (and in the work of some thinkers denies) the existence, or at least the benevolence of God, Pinn sees this position as a crucial heuristic tool for Black theology. For him it brings the Black experience to the fore of the conversation, allowing experience/reality to critique conventional religious symbols and beliefs. It is this claim (i.e., the privileging of Black experience over any religious symbol) that leads to a Christological problem for Christian thought – especially African American Christian thought.

The Christological Problem

> *"For God so loved the world that he gave his only Son, so that everyone who believes in him may not perish but may have eternal life."*[48]

This popular passage from the Gospel of John (along with several others) has been frequently interpreted as portraying the sufferings and death of Jesus as redemptive. God sacrificed God's only unique son in order to secure salvation for humanity. The necessity of Christ's suffering for redemption seems to be an undeniable fact of Christianity. The idea of "necessity" indicates the suffering of Jesus as intricate to God's plan of salvation, i.e. there seems to be a connection between suffering and glory.[49]

What can be gained from death, suffering, and pain? How do we relate to and worship a God who either permits or causes

---

[46] Ibid, p. 19.
[47] Ibid, p. 157.
[48] John 3:16 in *The New Oxford Annotated Bible, New Revised Standard Version, 3rd Edition*
[49] William J. O'Malley, *Redemptive Suffering: Understanding, Suffering, Living With It, Growing Through It* (New York, Y: The Crossroad Publishing Company, 1997), p. 117.

atrocities? My students and parishioners constantly asked questions like these when they experience instances of suffering, such as the loss of a loved one. On numerous occasions I have witnessed clergy consoling parishioners after the tragic death of a loved one by saying, "this was God's will" or "God did this for a reason." This kind of reasoning can be detrimental to spiritual growth and recovery after adversity.[50] Some theologians seek to develop a Christology that rejects the idea of redemptive suffering.[51] However, this leads to a christological problem. If we reject the principle of redemptive suffering, how do we interpret the death of Jesus the Christ? The essence of Christian faith seems to suggest Christ's death was to *redeem* humanity from sin.

An Adequate Alternative/Contemporary Understanding of Christology, Redemption, & Suffering

Both those who support and those who outright reject redemptive suffering have overlooked crucial christological themes. Both positions emphasize their particular aspect of Jesus' ministry and suffering that support their distinctive claims. For those who support redemptive suffering, the ministry and sufferings of Christ are chiefly about God's plan of salvation and/or Jesus' perfect fulfilling of God's will. Jesus suffering is extended to suffering in general. Suffering, then, is justified by the attribution of divine purpose. In one sense, this is essentially to provide meaning to suffering, i.e., people do not want to "suffer in vain." In another sense, this is to encourage faithfulness among believers in the face of inexplicable suffering. Those who reject the principle of redemptive suffering tend to emphasize the political and liberative aspect of Jesus' ministry and sufferings. While one would be hard-pressed to deny these political and liberative implications, an overemphasis can lead to the neglect of the salvific quality of Christ's life, death, and resurrection.

---

[50] We must acknowledge that for some the notion of redemptive suffering poses no crisis of faith. This present work, though, is for those who do find the notion of redemptive suffering troubling.

[51] Examples include Anthony Pinn and Delores Williams.

I wish to offer a three-prong solution to this Christological problem. Firstly, part of the problem lies in the interpretation and emphasis of Jesus' death by some Christian thinkers. There are those who focus on only this one element of Christ's saving work. The salvific work, however, encompasses the incarnation, life, ministry, death, burial, and resurrection of Jesus. We find evidence of this within the Christian tradition. Although Paul scarcely mentions explicit events, activities, or teachings from the ministry of Jesus, it is important to note that the teachings and actions of Jesus play a significant role in Pauline theology (including his soteriology).[52] For Irenaeus the incarnation is as important for salvation as the death and resurrection of Jesus Christ.[53] Through the incarnation, Christ fully identified with humanity and restored humanity to God by incorporating us into his obedience to God.[54] In essence, we participate in Christ's life, ministry, death, and resurrection.

It was through the incarnation, Jesus' teachings, ministry, death, and resurrection that a new covenant was established – one which included both Jews and Gentiles. Jesus was seeking the reconciliation of all humanity with God through his life, ministry, and even with his death. "When threatened with the cross, Jesus did not run or hide, attempting to avoid such an accursed death, but instead offered himself and his life to God with the implicit petition that what he had lived and died for might come to pass through him"[55] The salvific understanding of Jesus' death is shaped by this understanding as well. Jesus' death (and blood) was redeemed and justified, i.e., reconciled humanity to God, in the sense that it was because of Jesus' faithfulness, even unto death, along with his subsequent resurrection, that unquestionably

---

[52] See David Wenham, *Paul: Follower of Jesus or Founder of Christianity?* (Grand Rapids, MI: Eerdmans Press, 1995).
[53] Irenaeus, *Against Heresy* (Kessinger Publishing, 2004).
[54] Donald McKim, *Theological Turning Points: Major Issues in Christian Thought* (Atlanta, GA: John Knox Press, 1988), p. 80.
[55] David A. Brondos, *Fortress Introduction to Salvation and the Cross* (Minneapolis, MN: Fortress Press, 2007), p. 44.

obtained salvation for those who believed.[56] The emphasis on (and glorifying of) suffering is removed with a more comprehensive view of Jesus' saving work.

Secondly, we can recognize redeemable aspects from *instances* of suffering without maintaining that suffering (as a general category) is redemptive. In other words, we can work with God to try to produce some good out of malevolent and sinful instances of suffering. This is not to say suffering is a requirement of God for, say, spiritual growth or liberation. No instance of suffering is good or divinely inspired for pedagogical reasons. People seek to construct meaning and give reasons for suffering. They also seek to provide reasons that go beyond the immediate causes of suffering. Spiritual or divine value is assigned in order to sustain the notion that one does not or has not suffered in vain. We justify suffering by suggesting a divine *telos*. I see such justifications as mere constructions that are antithetical to the gospel and will of God. While I reject all such attempts to produce meaning and value in unmerited suffering, I realize liberation is possible in spite of suffering if we work with God to attain it. The effects of suffering can be surmounted when one engages in praxis against (and in spite of) evil and suffering.

There is nothing intrinsically good or redeemable in suffering. Instead, we have the capacity to shape and curtail the circumstances of suffering such that "some good" may come out of an unwarranted situation of affliction. This is possible only if those who are experiencing suffering participate in this transformation (to the best of their ability). We can say that suffering is redeemable in the sense that we act, in cooperation with God, to transform situations of suffering into situations of peace and the alleviation of suffering. In this sense, I concur with Anthony Pinn that "victories are not won because of or through suffering, but in spite of suffering."[57]

---

[56] Ibid, p. 45.
[57] Anthony Pinn, *Why Lord? Suffering and Evil in Black Theology*, p. 158.

Emilie Townes helps us in this regard. Townes' womanist ethics outright rejects any claim that suffering is God's will. The continual existence of suffering is an outrage. The aim of womanist ethics is the eradication of suffering based on the proposition that *the removal of suffering is God's redeeming purpose.* Embracing suffering diminishes the richness of the liberating love of God. Any discussion of suffering as good is a tool of oppression.[58] Based on the conceptual framework of Audre Lorde, Townes argues that one should move from the reactionary and powerless position of suffering to the transformative power of pain.[59] Lorde defined suffering as "unscrutinized and unmetabolized pain." Suffering removes the capacity of any oppressed individual or group to examine the conditions of their oppression.[60] Pain, on the other hand, is "an experience that must be recognized, named, and then used for transformation."[61] Lorde sees suffering as evil because it inhibits an individual's or a group's freedom to participate in means of liberation.[62] Pain substantiates those who are oppressed as loved children of God, names suffering as sin, and develops means to surmount it. If the resurrection of Jesus Christ is to be taken seriously, then this means that "true suffering" has been removed through the redemptive event of the resurrection – of which the empty cross and tomb bear witness.[63]

How is this expressed in terms of the cross and salvation? It is important to remember that nothing about Christ's suffering and death was pedagogical in nature. There was nothing for Jesus to learn through his sufferings. This fact eliminates all attempts to use Jesus' suffering and death as justification of other instances of suffering as pedagogical in nature. Christ's aim is the elimination of suffering. God removes suffering out of the world through the

---

[58] Emilie M. Townes, *Womanist Justice, Womanist Hope* (The American Academy of Religion, 1993), p. 197
[59] Ibid, pp. 195-196.
[60] Ibid, pp. 196-197
[61] Ibid, p. 194
[62] Ibid, p. 195
[63] Ibid, p. 195

life, ministry, death, and resurrection of Jesus. It is because of and through God's love that these actions are made available to all. All people can embrace the victory of the life, ministry, death, and resurrection of Jesus. Jesus' life and actions "moves the oppressed past suffering to pain and struggle." God has entered into history to "transform suffering into wholeness." Suffering is evil and is not representative of God's will or divine justice.[64] Transformation (via the movement from suffering to pain) is the divine act of moving a person or group from victim(s) to change agent(s).

Lastly, we can frame Christ's suffering and death on the cross as *the singular instance of redemptive suffering*. This proposition is acceptable with the caveat that it becomes non-operational outside of this singular instance of Jesus Christ's suffering and death for atonement (the reunion of God and humanity). Jesus' death has multiple dimensions and purposes, thus, it becomes operational in various ways. On the one hand, it is an example of oppressive powers seeking to crush a movement of liberation. Thus, Jesus' suffering is an appropriate and relevant model for the political and social realities of African Americans. On the other hand, Jesus' suffering and death is a component of the salvific act of God. There are redemptive qualities to Jesus suffering vis-a-vis the salvation and liberation of humanity. Jesus conquers death and suffering and evil by taking it onto himself. Jesus' suffering and death, however, does not supply justifications for forms of oppression and propagation of evil and suffering. The Christian tradition is consistent in the idea that Christ endures the cross so that others do not have to. Moreover, the death and suffering of Christ is non-operational as justification for oppression because only Christ had to endure that singular instance of suffering. For only the God-human can provide salvation.

The problem comes when theologians try to apply Christian metaphors to contemporary experiences, and the metaphor is extended further than it should. Metaphor refers to "understanding

---

[64] Ibid, p. 197

that is transferred 'over' from one thing to another."⁶⁵ A metaphor is possible when one thing has a similarity with another. The weight of the metaphor is based on the "is like" characteristics. We must remember, however, that the "is not like" is as important as the "is like."⁶⁶ A metaphor suggests something *is like* something but the two things are *not* identical. To lose sight of this can cause interpretive problems. When applying the metaphor of the Cross and/or the suffering of Jesus to African American experience of oppression the "is like" character is the political and socially oppression aspects surrounding Jesus' suffering and death. The crucifixion of Jesus Christ, for instance, has gained new meaning in the recent work of James Cone. His juxtaposition of the cross and the lynching tree offers a renewed model of how Black experience of suffering is mirrored in the gospel story.⁶⁷ Nonetheless, there are no redemptive qualities in this aspect of Jesus' sufferings.

The "is not like" aspect has to do with the salvific function of Jesus death. Christ's reconciliation of humanity to God has salvific connotations. The enslavement, torture, rape, and dehumanization of African Americans contain no salvific value. The continued racial aggressions through unjust political and social structures provide no redemptive qualities. If anything, the salvific nature of Jesus' suffering and death can serve only as a metaphor for reconciliation and establishing right (just) relations.⁶⁸

---

[65] Bernard Lee, *Jesus and the Metaphors of God: The Christs of the New Testament* (Mahwah, NJ: Paulist Press, 1993), p. 20.
[66] Ibid.
[67] A full –text version of Dr. Cone's lecture is available at http://larryjamesurbandaily.blogspot.com/2007/11/james-cone-cross-and-lynching-tree.html.
[68] Delores Williams, *Sisters in the Wilderness: The Challenge of Womanist God-Talk* (Maryknoll, NY: Orbis Press, 1993), pp. 164-165.

WORKS CITED

Augustine. *City of God*. New York: Penguin Classics, 2003.

Brondos, David A. *Fortress Introduction to Salvation and the Cross*. Minneapolis, MN: Fortress Press, 2007.

Carter, Earl. *No Apology Necessary*. Lake Mary, FL: Creation House, 1997.

Cone, James. *A Black Theology of Liberation*. Maryknoll, NY: Orbis Books, 1971.

Davis, Stephen, ed. *Encountering Evil*. Louisville, KY: Westminster John Knox Press, 2001.

Dews, Peter. *The Idea of Evil*. Malden, MA: Blackwell Publishing, 2007.

Hick, John. *Evil and the God of Love*. San Francisco, CA: Harper and Row Publishers, 1978.

Hume, David. *Dialogues Concerning Natural Religion 2nd Edition, Edited with an Introduction by Richard H. Popkin*. Indianapolis, IN: Hackett Publishing Company, 1998.

Irenaeus. *Against Heresies*. Whitefish, MT: Kessinger Publishing, 2004.

Lee, Bernard. *Jesus and the Metaphors of God: The Christs of the New Testament*. Mahwah, NJ: Paulist Press, 1993.

Leibniz, Gottfried Wilhelm. *Theodicy, Edited by Austin Farrar, Trans. by E. M. Huggard*. Charleston, SC: BiblioBazaar, 2007.

Mays, Benjamin. *The Negro's God*. New York, NY: Atheneum Publishing, 1938.

McBrien, Richard P. *Catholicism: New Study Edition*. New York, NY: HarperCollins Publishers, 1994.

McGill, Arthur C. *Suffering: A Test of Theological Method*. Philadelphia, PA: The Westminster Press, 2007.

McKim, Donald. *Theological Turning Points: Major Issues in Christian Thought*. Atlanta, GA: John Knox Press, 1988.

Mohler, James Aylward. *The Sacrament of Suffering: The Meeting of God and Man in Suffering Can Be A Way to Complete and Final Fulfillment*. Notre Dame, IN: Fides/Claretian, 1979.

Montgomery, Leslie. *Redemptive Suffering: Lessons Learned from the Garden of Gethsemane*. Wheaton, IL: Crossway Books, 2006.

Murphy, Larry G., ed. *Down By the Riverside: Readings in African American Religion*. New York, NY: New York University Press, 2000.

Neiman, Susan. *Evil in Modern Thought: An Alternative History of Philosophy*. Princeton, NJ: Princeton University Press, 2002.

O'Malley, William J. *Redemptive Suffering: Understanding, Suffering, Living With It, Growing Through It*. New York, NY: The Crossroad Publishing Company, 1997.

Pinn, Anthony. *Moral Evil and Redemptive Suffering: A History of Theodicy in African American Religious Thought*. Gainesville, FL: University of Florida Press, 2002.

Pinn, Anthony. *Why Lord? Suffering and Evil in Black Theology*. New York, NY: Continuum Press, 1995.

Quinn, Phillip L. and Charles Taliaferro, *A Companion to Philosophy of Religion*. Oxford, UK: Blackwell Publishing Ltd, 1997.

Roberts, J. Deotis. *Liberation and Reconciliation: A Black Theology*. Louisville, KY: Westminster John Knox Press, 2005.

Roberts, J. Deotis. *Black Religion, Black Theology: The Collected Essays of J. Deotis Roberts* Harrisburg, PA: Trinity Press International, 2003.

Swinton, John. *Raging With Compassion: Pastoral Responses to the Problem of Evil*. Grand Rapids, MI: William B. Eerdmans Publishing Company, 2007.

Thurman, Howard. *Jesus & the Disinherited*. Boston, MA: Beacon Press 1976.

Townes, Emilie M. *Womanist Justice, Womanist Hope*. Atlanta, GA: The American Academy of Religion, 1993.

Walker, David. *David Walker's Appeal: To the Coloured Citizens of the World*. University Park, PA: Pennsylvania State University Press, 2002.

Wenham, David. *Paul: Follower of Jesus or Founder of Christianity?* Grand Rapids, MI: Eerdmans Press, 1995.

Williams, Delores. *Sisters in the Wilderness: The Challenge of Womanist God-Talk*. Maryknoll, NY: Orbis Press, 1993.

Work, Telford. "Advent's Answer to the Problem of Evil." *International Journal of Systematic Theology* 2, no. 1 (March 2000): 100-111.

The Decline of Black Catholicism: What's Racial Slavery To Do With It?

Kwame Assenyoh, S.V.D.
Graduate Theological Union, Berkeley, CA

This essay links the current decline of black Catholicism to the racial slavery practiced in Roman Catholicism at its settlement in the USA. Employing missiological anthropological analysis, Assenyoh, S.V.D., argues that the racism that characterized the beginning of New World slavery remains in the Church and accounts for the decline of black Catholicism. Assenyoh calls for persistent critiques of racial slavery in the Church's history if there must be transformation rather than reformation.

"We're losing members steadily... and if we don't do something we're going to lose a lot more. ... The old injury has not been healed ... the church's long reluctance to condemn slavery."[1]

It is not the digger of a trench who sees its crookedness but the one who stands at the beginning of the trench and watches the digging.[2]

The two texts above capture the problem and the solution this article deals with. Sam Dennis' presents the fact that black Catholicism in the USA is in decline[3] and points to the unfinished

---

[1] Statement of Sam Dennis, a sociologist, quoted in Robert McClory, "Black and Catholic: Many Say They Are Faithful Despite Church's Inattention," *National Catholic Reporter* (March 13, 1998), http://findarticles.com/p/articles/mi_m1141/is_n19_v34/ai_20404493/pg_2/?tag=content;col1 (accessed June 30, 2009).
[2] Oral Tradition of the Ewe ethnic group in Ghana, West Africa.
[3] By decline I mean a dwindling in the number of members, especially the youth, their less participation even as they maintain their Catholic status, the closing down of black Catholic churches, ministries and programs, the acute drop in the number of black religious, clergy and lay leaders, and the more and more

problem of slavery as the locus of the solution. The second text – a saying among the Ewe ethnic group of South-eastern Ghana – suggests that we treat current problems from their origin or source location. Reactions to the decline vary. At least one black Catholic leader has left the Church in protest, and formed a church.[4] Others, who have rightly identified the problem of the decline and its causes as racism and slavery, have often fallen short of calling for structural transformation beyond mere reformation.[5] In the spirit of this Ewe saying, however, members of the black Catholic faith community, gathered in 1992 at the National Black Catholic Congress VII in New Orleans, Louisiana, made the following call:

---

disregard for cultural sensibility in the liturgical celebrations as well as leadership and membership formations of black Catholics. These have been widely reported by the following witnesses: Most Reverend Edward K. Braxton, "The View from the Barbershop; The Church and African-American Culture," *America* 178 (February 14, 1998): 1; William C. Leonard, "A Parish for the Black Catholics of Boston," *Catholic Historical Review* 83 (January 1997): 10; Arthur Jones, "Black Catholics: Life in a Chilly Church," *National Catholic Reporter* 34 (August 14, 1998); George Shuster and Robert M. Kearns, *Statistical Profile of Black Catholics*, with forward by Bernard Quinn, (Washington, D.C.: Josephite Pastoral Center, 1976), 39; See also, Robert McClory, "Black and Catholic."
[4] Teresa Malcolm, "Black Leader Leaves Church." *National Catholic Reporter* 33 (February 28, 1997), 8. Another article describes how rapidly younger African American Catholics are shedding the faith in which they were baptized while the hope of their parents (and adults) of a reversal of the declining trend fades (see Vivian R. Rouson, "Waiting for my Church to live its Creed – African American Catholic – Column," *National Catholic Reporter* (April 25, 1997), 13. See also Bryan Massingale, "Forty Years Later in a 'White Racist Institution': Looking Back, Looking Around, Looking Forward," Plenary Address of the 2008 Joint Conference of Black Clergy, Sisters, Deacons, and Seminarians, Montgomery, AL, July 29, 2008; Robert McClory, . "Black and Catholic: Many Say They Are Faithful Despite Church's Inattention." *National Catholic Reporter* 34, 13 March 1998,
http://findarticles.com/p/articles/mi_m1141/is_n19_v34/ai_20404493/ (accessed August 1, 2010).
[5] See the "erasing the color line" model by Albert J. Raboteau, "Relating Race and Religion: Four Historical Models," in *Uncommon Faithfulness: The Black Catholic Experience,* edited by M. Shawn Copeland, editor with LaReine-Marie Mosely and Albert J. Raboteau (Maryknoll, New York: Orbis Books, 2008), 14, 23f.

We suggest studies be conducted on the history of evangelization of [b]lack slaves. ... What models were used to evangelize? What were the personalities of those who evangelized like? What part did geography, politics, and the social climate play?[6]

The call was made because black Catholics were dissatisfied with the steady regression of black Catholicism in the USA.

I argue that racial slavery and ideology seriously and initially damaged the encounter between European Roman Catholicism and Africans, and that this damage remains responsible for the decline of US black Catholicism. Hence the paper suggests that black Catholics be persistent in calling for transformation of Church structures rather than reformation of the content of structures. The underlying assumption here is that slavery and racism were inextricably linked to Roman Catholic teaching for 1400 years.[7] Therefore, there is the need to place slavery and racism always at the center of the discussion on black Catholicism, particularly in the USA, and in the world in general.

I begin by examining the beginnings of the encounter between black people and Roman Catholicism in the New World,[8] and identify slavery as an expression of racism. In the second part I use Louis Luzbetak's missiological theory to draw the mission model inherent in the encounter, particularly in slavery, and how this model functioned in the Church's approach to black people from the ante-bellum through the reconstruction period. Part three considers how racism impacts specific events of the decline of

---

[6] Committee on African American Catholics, National Conference of Catholic Bishops, *Keep Your Hand on the Plow: The African American Presence in the Catholic Church* (Washington, DC: United States Catholic Conference, 1996), 103.
[7] See John F. Maxwell, *Slavery and the Catholic Church: The History of Catholic Teaching Concerning the Moral Legitimacy of the Institution of Slavery* (London/Chester: Barry Rose Publishers, 1975), 13.
[8] The New World here refers to the creation of the African Diaspora through the Atlantic Slave Trade (AST).

black Catholicism in our times. The conclusion suggests some action on the part of the Church in the path of repairing its mission model – a transformation of the Church's evangelization prospects, particularly in the African American.

Part One: The Beginnings – Slavery and Roman Catholics in the Americas

What was the cause of the Atlantic Slave Trade and slavery in the Americas? Was it economics or racial ideology? These are questions that preoccupied many historians of the AST and Black Studies scholars because the answer determines the kind of solution to the problem of slavery. Historical reports on European Roman Catholics' participation in slavery and the AST are uncontestable. Instead what follows here is a demonstration that, economic benefits not withstanding, racial ideology was the driving force of the slavery practiced by Roman Catholics in the Americas. This becomes clearer when we consider how significant the role of the Church was in the AST and slavery.

Roman Catholics and missionaries played a significant role more than the holding and using of slave labor. The Church's leadership and members were instrumental in the design and execution of the AST that led to the enslavement of African blacks in the New World.[9] In his famous work, *Capitalism and Slavery*,

---

[9] I distinguish between slavery and the AST since, according to testimonies of many scripture and history scholars, slavery existed in ancient times, in the Old Testament, in the New Testament, and through the Middle Ages to our times. Slavery also existed in almost all societies; see Paul E. Lovejoy, *Transformations in Slavery: A History of Slavery in Africa*, 2nd ed., (Cambridge: Cambridge University Press, 2000), 1; Joseph E. Inikori, "Slaves or Serfs? A Comparative Serfdom in Europe and Africa," in *The African Diaspora: African Origins and New World Identities,* edited by Isidore Okpewho et al., (Bloomington, Indiana: Indiana University Press, 2001), 51; Maxwell, *Slavery and the Catholic Church*, 22ff. I will limit the scope of the Church's role in slavery, however, to pre-modern, modern and our contemporary times, that is, from the 15th to the 21st Centuries. This is because it is within this period that the Atlantic slave trade – "the slavery that … evolved during the Renaissance, Reformation, and Enlightenment" – occurred; see David Eltis, *The Rise of African Slavery in the Americas* (Cambridge: Cambridge University Press, 2000), 8.

black scholar and first prime minister of Trinidad and Tobago Eric Williams noted that the "[o]rigin of Negro Slavery" in the New World was coterminous with "bitter" struggles over lands for economic prosperity among Catholic European colonial countries: Portugal and Spain.[10] The Papal bulls of 1455 and 1497 triggered these "rival claims" for economic opportunities because, in these bulls, the pope assigned non-European lands in Africa and the Americas to Portugal and Spain respectively with a *mission* – "to reduce to servitude all infidel peoples."[11] Countries like England, France, and Holland challenged the pope's authority to assign such lands and joined the dispute to fight for their share and place in the economic advantages of the New World. In this context and place of battle for power and economic wealth by Europeans, "The Negro, too," Williams maintains, "was to have his place, though he did not ask for it: it was the broiling sun of the sugar, tobacco and cotton plantations of the New World."[12] Williams concluded that slavery was the result of capitalism, a position that has enjoyed some support among contemporary scholars.[13]

It is clear that Williams drew his conclusion from his focus on the European countries' imperial, conquering, and mercantile activities in his analysis. However scholars today who challenge Williams' conclusion focus on the significant role of papal bull discourses and their execution by missionaries in the launching of the New World slavery. V. Y. Mudimbe reports his analysis on one of the bulls of pope Nicholas V, *Dum Diversas* (1452) as follows:

> *Dum Diversas* clearly stipulates [the] right to invade, conquer, expel, and fight *(invadendi, conquirendi, expugnandi, debellandi)* Muslims, pagans and other enemies of Christ. ... Christian kings, following the

---

[10] See Eric Williams, *Capitalism and Slavery* (New York: Russell and Russell, 1944), 3-4.
[11] Ibid., 3.
[12] Ibid., 4.
[13] See for example, Oliver C. Cox, "Race Relations: Its Meaning, Beginning, and Process," in *Theories of Race and Racism: A Reader*, 2nd edition, edited by Les Back and John Solomos (New York: Routledge, 2009), 78.

> Pope's decisions, could enter pagan kingdoms ... and dispossess them of their personal property, land, and whatever they might have *(et mobilia et immobilia bona quaecumque per eos detenta ac possessa).* The king and his successors have the power and right to put these peoples into perpetual slavery *(subjugandi illorumque personas in perpetuam servitutem).*[14]

From his analyses of such papal bulls and missionary discourses as the above, Mudimbe discovers a three-stage scheme he refers to as "the concepts of derision, refutation-demonstration, and orthodoxy-conformity."[15] The language of the bulls first derided – ethnocentrically misrepresented - the religion and culture of Africans; second, it refuted by European rational arguments – the task of theology to convince Africans themselves to reject their own culture; and finally, the discourse of the bulls imposed European norms as orthodox in non-European lands.[16] Mudimbe demonstrates that this scheme, which opened the way for Europeans to invent, invade and enslave "Africa," was both ideological and racial.

Despite their different conclusions, the analyses of both Williams and Mudimbe show that the Roman Catholic Church, through its racial and ideological scheme, played an original role in landing Europeans in Africa for the purpose of enslavement. Indeed, the Atlantic Slave Trade that saw the forced migration of Africans in the Americas was an offshoot of an initial racial and ideological scheme embedded in papal and missionary discourses of the 15th and 16th centuries.

Racial slavery therefore continued to characterize the contact between African blacks and the initial faces of the Roman Catholic Church in the Americas. Black Catholic scholars have also made

---

[14] V. Y. Mudimbe, *The Invention of Africa: Gnosis, Philosophy, and the Order of Knowledge* (Bloomington: Indiana University Press, 1988), 45.
[15] Ibid., 52.
[16] Ibid., 52-53.

their contributions to the question of the Church's role in the enslavement of black people in the US. An historical research with depth on this issue by Cyprian Davis is found in *The History Black Catholics in the United States*. Davis' account reveals that although there were black people who made significant contributions to the early Catholic settlings[17] in the Americas, racial biases and perceptions on the part of the Europeans led to two forms of treatment of black people. First, racial perception of Europeans Catholics on blacks was manifested in an intentional devaluation, distortion, and neglect of the black presence and contributions in the discovery and founding of the church in the Americas. This was evident in Davis' account of Esteban, who was "the first black man to traverse what is now the territory of the United States" in 1536.[18] He was a slave of Moroccan origin who had escaped capture and was the only black man among the first four Spaniards who came to the New World "in an expedition that had evangelization of the Indians as one of its goals."[19] However, as Davis points out, very little is known about his accomplishments. So also before the establishment of the Spanish colony in the territory of today's Florida, Davis also underlines the active contribution of Spanish-speaking blacks that have gone without acknowledgement.[20]

The second effect of the racial perception of Europeans on blacks, to be drawn from Davis' account, is a systematic domination and oppression of blacks, of which slavery was a central characteristic. The centrality and importance of black peoples' enslavement are reflected in the banality of the practice in all rank and file of the Roman Catholic Church in the years of the

---

[17] Cyprian Davis, *The History of Black Catholics in the United States* (New York: The Crossroad Publishing Company, 1996), 28.
[18] Ibid.
[19] Ibid., 28-29.
[20] Ibid., 29-30. Also, in the second Spanish period (cir. 1784-1821) the eleven families who founded the city of Los Angeles – Nuestra Senora de Los Angeles as it was called at its foundation – were said to be all Catholic of whom "over half were black, two were Spanish and the rest were Indians" (Ibid., 33), but as in many other cities the "black element" were neglected and were made to eventually "evolved into mestizos and Indians."

country's foundation. The very first American bishop, John Carroll, Davis reports, "was a slave owner" and so were others. In Maryland, "by the end of the seventeenth century, the Jesuits had introduced on their lands African slaves,"[21] and:

> [I]n 1836 the general of the Jesuits, John Roothaan, approved the sale of slaves; provided the practice of the Catholic faith by the slaves was assured and the families were not separated. In 1837 Thomas Mulledy became provincial, and ... [a]ltogether 272 slaves from the Jesuit estates in southern Maryland were sold to purchasers in Louisiana. They were not necessarily sold to Catholic slave-owners, and in the end families were separated.[22]

Many other religious and missionary communities in the American Catholic church are cited in Davis' report as participating in enslaving black people.[23] So entrenched was the practice of slavery in Roman Catholicism that the bishops of the US Catholic Church resisted the calls and efforts of the world to abolish slavery. The basic notions that fueled this attitude of Catholics against their fellow Catholics of African descent were articulated by Bishop William Henry Elder. He held that "the African American slave was part child, part animal, part saint,"[24] and those who were sympathetic to slaves still described them as "inferior both intellectually and physically."[25]

The conclusion Davis draws is that, as it did on the civil society of the United States, so did slavery cast a shadow over the history of American Catholicism, so that slavery is connected to Roman Catholic history. This clearly reflects the conclusion we drew from the analyses of Williams and Mudimbe earlier that racial slavery was coterminous with Roman Catholicism in the 15th and 16th centuries. Davis' account goes further to reveal that

---

[21] Ibid., 36.
[22] Ibid., 37; See also, James T. Fisher, *Communion of Immigrants: A History of Catholics in America* (Oxford: Oxford University Press, 2002), 53.
[23] Davis, *The History of Black Catholics*, 35-39.
[24] Ibid., 44.
[25] Ibid., 61.

there was continuity of the initial relation between Roman Catholicism and black slavery into the settling of the USA.

Part Two: Missiological Implications of Racial Slavery

What then was the mission approach of Roman Catholicism toward black people in the United States after the abolition of slavery? I seek to demonstrate here that, owing to the profound embedding of racial ideology in Roman Catholicism, the abolishing of slavery did not eliminate racism. In other words the missionary approach of the Church toward black people in the reconstruction era retained the spirit of 15th and 16th century papal and missionary discourses. The mission models of the Church in the time of slavery continued well into the reconstruction era.

Catholic Mission Models in the Antebellum Era

According to Louis Luzbetak, theoretically, there are three categories into which mission models may be grouped based on the revelation of their "dominant traits."[26] First, there are models whose dominant traits are ethnocentric oriented. A second group of models has "accommodational orientation" and a third group is contextual or "incarnational" or "inculturational" in their orientations. Luzbetak's explanation of these categories of models helps us to assign or relate the ethnocentrically oriented category of mission models to the context of the encounter between black people in the United States and the Roman Catholic Church. This may help to explain the contents of the context, that is, the enslavement of blacks by whites.

Luzbetak attempts a definition of ethnocentrism thus:

> Ethnocentrism is a tendency (to some degree present in every human being) to regard the ways and values of one's own society as *the* normal, right, proper, and certainly the best way of thinking, feeling, speaking, and doing things, whether it be in regard to eating, sleeping, dressing,

---

[26] Louis J. Luzbetak, *The Church and Cultures: A New Perspective in Missiological Anthropology* (Maryknoll, NY: Orbis Books, 1988), 64.

disposing of garbage, marrying, burying the dead, or speaking with God.²⁷

The concept of ethnocentrism, therefore, simply refers to normalizing, generalizing, or universalizing what pertains to one's own context, particularity or situation. As a process of socialization by which the young of a society or people are equipped to participate and to survive, enculturation makes ethnocentrism almost impossible to undo or change. Enculturation solidifies and instills in a person the ethos and worldview with their constituent values, beliefs, and perceptions of reality. Ethnocentrism, according to Luzbetak, manifests itself in three major forms – paternalism, triumphalism, and racism.²⁸

These three forms of ethnocentrism characterized the attitude of European Roman Catholics who first came to the New World as explorers, missionaries, lay, religious or clergy as we have seen above. European ethnocentrism in its paternalistic form enabled some of these early Euro-American Catholics to rationalize the moral contradiction of being Christians and holding and trading in slaves. As Davis writes, Bishop Auguste Marie Martin of Natchitoches in northern Louisiana held that "slavery is really a disguised blessing for the Africans, 'children of the race of Canaan,' for through slavery they have received the faith and other advantages."²⁹ Bevans and Schroeder also agree that the "Jesuit Reductions Model" of mission failed because of its paternalism.³⁰ This is exactly how Luzbetak explains paternalism: "a misguided compassion that tends to humiliate the would-be beneficiary, making them even more dependent on the would-be benefactor than they were before."³¹ Triumphalistic ethnocentrism is a conviction that one's culture or the Church's success gives it the right to spread their success and force others to receive them.

---

²⁷ Ibid., 65.
²⁸ Ibid.
²⁹ Davis, *The History of Black Catholic*, 51.
³⁰ Stephen B. Bevans and Roger P. Schroeder, *Constants in Context: A Theology of Mission for Today* (Maryknoll: Orbis Books, 2004), 183.
³¹ Luzbetak, *The Church and Cultures*, 65-66.

Finally, Luzbetak presents racist ethnocentrism as an orientation for some mission models.[32] In his view, this category of models also generates classicism in society. It is the model that maintains that "[t]he color of the skin somehow condemns certain 'less fortunate' individuals to second-class citizenship, not only in society at large but sometimes in the Church as well."[33] Black Catholic theologian Jamie Phelps writes that the Catholic Church's ministry in antebellum times was held from black slaves and free people as it was a matter of official church policy.[34] It was, she goes on to say, rather reserved for "the immigrant Catholics of European decent with whom most of the clergy and bishops could claim a cultural and racial identity."[35] I single racism out for elucidation separately in order to critique Luzbetak. His presentation treats all three as though they were mutually exclusive forms of ethnocentrism. It may not however be Luzbetak's position or intention to make paternalism, triumphalism and racism as exclusive forms of the same reality. There is no mention of their interrelatedness, hence my critique.

It is important then to point out the position of Michael Omi and Howard Winart on racism. From what they call the "racial formation perspective" Omi and Winart advance that the concept of racism has to do with the creation and reproduction "of structures of domination based on essentialist categories of race."[36] In this sense race is conceived of as a neutral fluid term that is socio-historically constructed; but racism is the use of this socio-historical term for domination and oppression. This is the hermeneutic of race and racism that I adopt in this paper. Slavery then was a kind of domination that had its origin in racism. In fact

---

[32] See Luzbetak, 66.
[33] Ibid.
[34] Jamie T. Phelps, "The Mission Ecclesiology of John R. Slattery: A Study of an African-American Mission of the Catholic Church in the Nineteenth Century," unpublished doctoral dissertation, Catholic University of American, 1989, 85.
[35] Ibid.
[36] Michael Omi and Howard Winart, *Racial Formation in the United States: From the 1960s to the 1990s* (New York: Routledge, 1994), 71.

Omi and Winart and other African American and Black Diaspora Studies theorists, though not unanimously, now hold that racism morphed through different periods in human history manifesting itself in different institutions and practices.[37] Hence, we can see racism not just as one of the ethnocentric forms, but as an embedding dynamic in both paternalism and triumphalism inasmuch as these forms conceal the domination of others based on something they consider as essentially different in the humanity of these others. This has cultural implications for both the slave-owners and the oppressed slaves. The former on one hand, not only assert their culture but also, as a superior culture, normalize, universalize and generalize it. The latter, on the other hand, do not just have their culture impoverished, but also this impoverished culture is assimilated gradually until it falls out of existence in the face of the dominant culture.

The significance of re-conceptualizing racism and race in this way is to make way for our understanding of the black Catholic experience in relation to the ethnocentric model of mission in the antebellum and the reconstruction periods of the United States. We have seen extensively the context of black Catholics in the ante-bellum period as a context where racism, embedded in triumphalism and paternalism, manifested itself in the form of slavery.

Catholic Mission Models and Black Catholics in the Reconstruction Era

This post-war period in black history was a period of reconstruction for both the nation (as a recovery from the war) and black people in general as a reconstruction of their lives as free citizens of the nation. Moreso for black Catholics it was to be a period of reconstructing their Catholic faith in all its dimensions. Black Catholics, both formerly enslaved or never enslaved alike, took the opportunity of the relative physical freedom to make strides in the Roman Catholic Church. Some examples of the

---

[37] See Ibid.

achievements made by the lay black Catholics, reported by Davis, include the establishment of black Catholic lay organizations, the formation of black religious communities, the promotion of education for black children and the emergence of black Catholic clergy. These achievements of black Catholics however were not made without struggle. This is because the post-Civil War context was one in which the pastors of the Church neglected the blacks by denying them pastoral care, religious education and evangelization, leadership, and so on. A meeting organized to work out "a policy on the national level for ministry and evangelization of the former slaves," one year after the war, produced "no coherent policy."[38]

According to Davis, before this period, there had been complaint letters sent to Rome on behalf of black people to petition the pope for missionaries for apostolic work among black Catholics since the white Euro-American Catholic clergy had rejected pastoral work among blacks. The letter of one Harriet Thompson in 1853 lays out the pastoral situation and struggle of black Catholics in those days.[39] The fundamental problem that the black community faced in the Reconstruction period, as it stands out in Thompson's letter, was the neglect of the black community by the local clergy and religious. Davis does not mention a reply from Rome to Thompson's letter but he believes that this pre-civil war letter played a role in a later intervention for the sake of the evangelization of black people. Rather than working with and among the blacks themselves, the bishops of the United States preferred soliciting from people they disagreed with on the question of the abolition of slavery and the Slave Trade, especially Irish "missionaries from Europe to work among the black population."[40] Delores Labbé reports that in southern

---

[38] Davis, *The History of Black Catholics*, 116.
[39] Ibid., 94.
[40] Ibid., 120; From my 8-year pastoral experience I learn that, even today, especially in the Archdiocese of New Orleans, more and more white diocesan priests stay away from serving as pastor in African American Catholic Churches – churches that are predominantly black. Most white pastors of African American Churches are members of religious orders. The common reason for this is that the

Louisiana, a system of "segregated parishes" for blacks was experimented with to see if it would be effective in curbing or dealing with the racial tension of the period after the Civil War. However, she points out, that "the experiment of the 1890's has become the dilemma of the 1970's"[41] because what was put on experimental basis became the norm filling southern Louisiana with many segregated "white churches" and "black churches" that still exist today. It was because the bishops, most of whom benefited from slavery and the Slave Trade, felt "resentment ... toward the freed slaves after the Civil War"[42] that brought the emancipation. From the above, we can conclude that the white Catholic leadership's decision and negative attitude towards black evangelization in the reconstruction period was ethnocentrically driven. To employ Omi and Winart's racial formation perspective, the bishops' approach to the mission among black people in those days was fundamentally "racist", a "racist project", or simply, "racism."

Part Three: Racial Slavery and the Decline of Black Catholicism

To say that black Catholicism in the United States is on the decline in our contemporary times is not hard to verify. The widely reported events include the closing of black Catholic inner-city schools and churches for lack of funds and diocesan personnel, the dwindling number of black vocations to the

---

income of predominantly black parishes is not enough to maintain a diocesan priest. Diocesan priests need their salaries as they are registered with Internal Revenue Service (IRS) as "self-employed" and eligible to file taxes on their income. Religious order members do not personally receive income but their communities do. In my view, however, the fact that bishops could support their priests, as religious orders do, in poorer parishes if they regard it important, makes the old reason – racism that has trickled down from the post-war white leadership sentiments regarding evangelization of blacks – a probable explanation.

[41] Delores E. Labbé, *Jim Crow Comes to Church: The Establishment of Segregated Catholic Parishes in South Louisiana* (New York: Arno Press, 1978), 92.
[42] Ibid., 121.

priesthood and religious life, and the estrangement of black philosophical and theological scholarship from the day-to-day black Catholic communitarian experience.

The most recent report that strongly makes the connection between the decline of black Catholicism of our time, the practice of racial slavery of old, and racial discrimination was delivered by the black Catholic ethicist Bryan Massingale. In his 2008 Plenary Address of the Joint Conference of Black Clergy, Sisters, Deacons and Seminarians at Montgomery, Alabama, Massingale spoke of the frustration and disappointment brewing in the black Catholic community as it witnesses a free-fall after many years of promises by the hierarchy of the Church. He presented a recent study that shows, "only 18% of the country's bishops have issued statements condemning the sin of racism." Since the bishops' conference collectively published their pastoral letter on racism, *Brothers and Sisters to Us*, "over half of ...[diocesan] offices of black Catholics report that they lack the financial resources needed for effective ministry in the [b]lack community;" "[b]lack enrollment in Catholic elementary and high schools has declined in the past 20 years, while Asian and Hispanic enrollment has increased;" and the "... [w]hite Catholics over the last twenty-five years exhibit diminished – rather than increased – support for government policies aimed at reducing racial equality."[43] The common lesson in the report is what this paper suggests – that the racism of slavery is alive and well in the Church. As Massingale puts it:

> [W]e have not yet fully appreciated the profound implications of our founding insight: the U.S. Catholic church is a 'white racist institution.' ... What makes it 'white' and 'racist' is the pervasive belief that European aesthetics, music, theology, and persons – and only these – are standard, normative, universal, and truly 'Catholic.'[44]

---

[43] Bryan N. Massingale, "Forty Years Later in a 'White Racist Institution': Looking Back, Looking Around, Looking Forward," Plenary Address of the 2008 Joint Conference of Black Clergy, Sisters, Deacons and Seminarians, Montgomery, AL, July 29, 2008. See also Conference Committee on African American Catholics, online at www.usccb.org/saac.

[44] Ibid., 15, 16.

The profound nature of the problem requires blacks to adopt an equal and profound approach to deal with it.

Thus Rodney Petersen writes:

> Orlando Patterson summarizes the toll that racism took upon a people. He cites broken bloodlines with their impact upon gender relations, crises in marriage and family life among African-Americans. The impact upon images of masculinity and patterns of social accountability are further described. All of this bears itself out in current crime statistics. The effect of racist social reality on upon the youth of America is detailed in its chilling reality by Fred Smith.[45]

These effects of racism may be applicable also to black Catholics. First, in the antebellum period, slavery allowed white Catholic slave-owners to sell their slaves. The selling of slaves was widely known to be an immediate cause of destruction to the black-slave-family because of the separation of relatives. There is also the destructive effect of racism through slavery on black men, women, and their interrelationship that disorganized the socio-cultural life of the black community. Finally, Petersen's quote also mentions black youth as one of the casualties of racism. Through slavery the youth – children of slaves – were slaves. They suffered from the lack of education and lack of self-worth with the consciousness that they belonged to an inferior, powerless, and hopeless race. All these, together, disturb the self image of young blacks and affect the way they interact with the world and their immediate environment – family, friends, neighborhood, society, etc.. Petersen seeks to stress that the extent of the destructive effects of racism (seen through slavery) is genocidal – it destroys a people because it destroys everyone in the black family without exception. Blacks who lived in the post-Civil War era did not

---

[45] Rodney L. Petersen, "Mission in the Context of Racism, Restorative Justice and Reconciliation" in *Antioch Agenda: Essays on the Restorative Church in Honor of Orlando E. Costas,* ed. Daniel Jeyaraj et al, (New Delhi: Indian Society for the Promotion of Christian Knowledge, 2007), 263.

encounter racism in the form of slavery; instead, they suffered under white paternalistic and triumphalistic models of mission in the Catholic Church.

The decline of Catholicism among blacks in the USA should not be a surprising phenomenon. It should be expected because of the ever-lingering racial ideology in Roman Catholicism in the USA. Racism reminds black people about slavery and threatens to conquer, dispossess, and dominate as the papal bulls declared. Racism then creates insecurity of membership in black Catholics as their culture and gifts are, in Mudimbe's terms, derided, refuted and replaced by European cultural forms as orthodox. Racism's importance made it a central issue for most black Catholic conferences. The first three National Black Catholic Congresses during Reconstruction called the bishops' attention to racial discrimination and the need for inclusion or redress.[46] In 1984, ten black bishops issued a pastoral letter on evangelization entitled "What We Have Seen and Heard" in which they underlined racism as an obstacle to evangelization.[47] And in 2002, the National Black Catholic Congress IX took place in Chicago, where a national pastoral plan was designed which again featured an urgent call to the US Catholic leadership to focus on the elimination of "racism" especially in all parish levels.[48] Shawn Copeland vividly puts it that "pastoral neglect and disregard by white clergy and hierarchy have forced black Catholics to seek out separate sites for the development of our own spiritual life."[49]

---

[46] The American Catholic Tradition, *Three Catholic Afro-American Congresses* (Cincinnati, OH: The American Catholic Tribune, 1978), 14.
[47] See "What We Have Seen and Heard: A Pastoral Letter on Evangelization From the Black Bishops of the United States" online at www.aodonline.org/NR/rdonlyres/.../seenandheard.pdf (accessed December 11, 2008).
[48] The National Black Catholic Congress, "National Black Catholic Congress IX" online at http://www.nbccongress.org/aboutus/nbcc-congresses/congress-09-PRINCIPAL-SPIRITUALITY.asp (accessed December 11, 2008).
[49] M. Shawn Copeland, "'Catholic Theology: African American Context,' 1998," in *"Stamped with the Image of God": African Americans as God's Image in Black,* edited by Cyprian Davis, O.S.B. and Jamie Phelps, O.P. (Maryknoll, New York: Orbis Books, 2003), 148.

She goes on to point out what she sees as the decline of black Catholicism namely: "[t]he thwarted work of the black Catholic congresses of the nineteenth century, the collapse of the Federated Colored Catholics in the early twentieth century, the demise of Catholic schools in so many cities, along with the mergers and closures of so many parishes that nurtured black Catholics ... ."[50] Copeland explicitly makes the case that the decline of black Catholicism is a direct result of racism. One may ask whether the Church did nothing good toward blacks? The church made some strides in individual cases; however the critique of this paper concerns the Church's stance on racism in its structures and the issue of slavery, which seriously damaged and marred its ministry to black people. At best, most scholars describe the Church's approach to issues of black people as one carried out in reluctance and ambiguity.[51]

Conclusion

According to Bevans and Schroeder, "The history of mission, the movements of culture, and the history of theology intersect, and depending on the *way* they intersect, various 'models' of mission can be discerned."[52] Analogously, it expected that if any of these three changes, the rest must change as well. However this did not happen. While the history of the antebellum period and the slave cultural practices were changed, the theology has not been changed because, to use J. Deotis Roberts' words, "we have not dealt racism [the ideology that fuels the theology] a mortal blow here at home in the United States."[53] In his book *Race: A Theological Account*, J. Kameron Carter expresses surprise:

---

[50] Ibid.
[51] Wright, "Black Liberation and the Catholic Church," 75; see also Bentley R. Anderson, "Black, White, and Catholic: Southern Jesuits Confront the Race Question, 1952," *Catholic Historical Review* 91, no. 3 (July 2005): 484. See also John F. Quinn, "Three Cheers for the Abolitionist Pope!: American Reaction to Gregory XVI's Condemnation of the Slave Trade, 1840-1860," *Catholic Historical Review* 90, no. 1 (January 2004): 85.
[52] Bevans and Schroeder, *Constants in Context*, 73.
[53] J. Deotis Roberts, *Black Theology in Dialogue* (Philadelphia: The Westminster Press, 1987), 13.

> [T]hat modern racial discourse and practice have their genesis inside Christian theological discourse and missiological practice, which themselves were tied to the practice of empire in the advance of Western civilization. But it is precisely an account of this problem that is sorely lacking.[54]

This implies that, in order to change or transform its missionary approach to black people in the USA, the Roman Catholic Church must seriously confront its historical, theological, and cultural interpretations, perceptions or beliefs about black people. In this paper I have focused on the historical and cultural interpretation expressed in the ethnocentric orientation of white Catholic leaders toward blacks since the inception of the Church in the United States. The call of the black Catholic Church is a call for transformation, not reformation. I find missiologist Keith Bridston's view of mission in the ecumenical movement era appropriate for the present discourse. He writes:

> The idea that a reformation of mission would be an adequate change fails to take into account the possibility that the traditional forms of mission are themselves irreformable because they embody a response to a world that no longer exists and express a theological understanding of the relation of the world to God that is now felt to be fallacious.[55]

It means black Catholics must not shy away from insisting on structural changes; nor should we settle for reforms of the contents of structures. As Emilie Townes warns, concerning civil society, "failure to engage structurally in the age of empire has been and will continue to be disastrous ..." if we acquiesce in reforms.[56]

---

[54] J. Kameron Carter, *Race: A Theological Account* (Oxford: Oxford University Press, 2008), 3.
[55] Keith Bridston, *Mission Myth and Reality* (New York: Friendship Press, 1965), 17.
[56] Emilie M. Townes, *Womanist Ethics and the Cultural Production of Evil* (New York: Palgrave Macmillan, 2006), 126.

Slavery and the slave trade must be seriously studied, analyzed and incorporated into our theologizing. The sin of slavery will not be appeased until the US Church openly apologizes to blacks as a starting point of a healing process that would include a systematic and open condemnation of the theological and ethical teachings in the past – teachings that have discretely informed structures in the Church, theological academies, and seminaries.[57] When he was recently interviewed, an old black priest who has experienced racial discrimination all his life was asked, "Right now, today, what would you like to see the church doing that you don't perceive it to be doing?" His answer: "For one thing, I haven't heard the church say 'I'm sorry' publicly for all the things that have happened and are still happening to black people."[58] Without transformation in the variables, the mission model(s) of today's Church will continue to be ethnocentric, and will yield the same failed and declining results in black Catholicism of today.

---

[57] See Kwame Nantamhu, "Question of Apology for Slavery: A Global View," Trinicenter.com (June 15, 2001), http://www.trinicenter.com/kwame/20010615d.htm (accessed September 16, 2009); Philip S. Kaufman, *Why You Can Disagree and Remain a Faithful Catholic*, foreword by Richard A. McCormick, (New York: The Crossroad Publishing Company, 1995), 48.

[58] John L. Allen Jr., "Black Priest Lives with Hope, Resignation," *National Catholic Reporter* 34 (November 21, 1997).

WORKS CITED

Allen, John L. Jr. "Black Priest Lives with Hope, Resignation." *National Catholic Reporter* 34 (November 21, 1997).

Bevans, Stephen B. and Roger P. Schroeder. *Constants in Context: A Theology of Mission for Today.* American Society of Missiology Series, No. 30. Maryknoll, New York: Orbis Books, 2004.

Black Bishops of the United States. "What We Have Seen and Heard." A Pastoral Letter on Evangelization. Online at www.aodonline.org/NR/rdonlyres/.../seenandheard.pdf (accessed December 11, 2008).

Braxton, Edward K. "The View from the Barbershop: The Church and African-American Culture." *America,* 178: 18-22 (February 14, 1998).

Bridston, Keith. *Mission Myth and Reality.* New York: Friendship Press, 1965.

Carter, J. Kameron. *Race: A Theological Account.* Oxford: Oxford University Press, 2008.

Committee on African American Catholics, National Conference of Catholic Bishops. *Keep You're Hand on the Plow: The African American Presence in the Catholic Church.* Washington, D.C.: United States Catholic Conference, 1996.

Copeland, Shawn M. "Body, Race, and Being." In Serene Jones and Paul Lakeland, eds.,*Constructive Theology: A Contemporary Approach to Classical Themes.* Minneapolis: Fortress Press, 2005.

-----. "'Catholic Theology: African American Context,' 1998." In Cyprian Davis, O.S.B. and Jamie Phelps, O.P., eds., *"Stamped with the Image of God": African Americans as God's Image in Black.* Maryknoll, New York: Orbis Books, 2003.

Cox, Oliver C. "Race Relations: Its Meaning, Beginning, and Process." In *Theories of Race and Racism: A Reader,* 2nd

edition, ed. Les Back and John Solomos, 71-78. New York: Routledge, 2009.

Davis, Cyprian. *The History of Black Catholics in the United States.* New York: The Crossroad Publishing Company, 1996.

Eltis, David. *The Rise of African Slavery in the Americas.* Cambridge: Cambridge University Press, 2000.

Fisher, James T. *Communion of Immigrants: A History of Catholics in America.* New York: Oxford University Press, 2002.

Hood, Robert E. *Begrimed and Black: Christian Traditions on Blacks and Blackness.* Minneapolis: Fortress Press, 1994.

Inikori, Joseph E. "Slaves or Serfs? A Comparative Serfdom in Europe and Africa." In *The African Diaspora: African Origins and New World Identities,* ed. Isidore Okpewho et al.. Bloomington, IN: Indiana University Press, 2001).

Jones, Arthur. "Black Catholics: Life in a Chilly Church." *National Catholic Reporter* 34 (August 14, 1998), http://findarticles.com/p/articles/mi_m1141/is_n36_v34/ai_21229851/ (accessed August 1, 2010).

Kaufman, Philip S. *Why You Can Disagree and Remain a Faithful Catholic, foreword by Richard A. McCormick* New York: The Cross Publishing Company, 1995.

Labbé, Dolores, E. *Jim Crow Comes to Church: The Establishment of Segregated Catholic Parishes in South Louisiana.* Second Edition. New York: Arno Press, 1978.

Leonard, William C. "A Parish for the Black Catholics of Boston." *Catholic Historical Review* 83 (January 1997): 10.

Lovejoy, Paul E. *Transformations in Slavery: A History of Slavery in Africa, 2nd ed.* Cambridge: Cambridge University Press, 2000).

Luzbetak, Louis J. *The Church and Cultures: New Perspectives in Missiological Anthropology.* Forward by Eugene Nida. Maryknoll, New York: Orbis Books, 1988.

Malcolm, Teresa. "Black Leader Leaves Church." *National Catholic Reporter* 33 (28 February 1997), 8.

Massingale, Bryan N. "Forty Years Later in a 'White Racist Institution': Looking Back, Looking Around, Looking Forward." Plenary Address of the 2008 Joint Conference of Black Clergy, Sisters, Deacons, and Seminarians, Montgomery, AL, July 29, 2008.

Maxwell, John F. *Slavery and the Catholic Church: The History of Catholic Teaching Concerning the Moral Legitimacy of the Institution of Slavery*. London/Chester: Barry Rose Publishers, 1975.

McClory, Robert. "Black and Catholic: Many Say They Are Faithful Despite Church's Inattention." *National Catholic Reporter* 34 (13 March 1998) http://findarticles.com/p/articles/mi_m1141/is_n19_v34/ai_20404493/ (accessed August 1, 2010).

Mudimbe, V. Y. *The Invention of Africa: Gnosis, Philosophy, and the Order of Knowledge*. Bloomington: Indiana University Press, 1988.

Nantumbe, Kwame. "Question of Apology for Slavery: Global View." Trinicenter.com (June 15, 2001), http://www.trinicenter.com/kwame/20010615d.htm (accessed September 16, 2009).

Omi, Michael and Howard Winant. *Racial Formation in the United States: From the 1960s to the 1990s*. 2nd ed. New York/London: Routledge, 1994.

Peterson, Rodney L. "Mission in the Context of Racism, Restorative Justice and Reconciliation." In Daniel Jeyaraj et al., eds., *Antioch Agenda: Essays on the Restorative Church in Honor of Orlando E. Costas*. New Delhi: Indian Society for the Promotion of Christian Knowledge, 2007.

Phelps, Jamie T., O.P. "The Mission Ecclesiology of John R. Slattery: A Study of an African-American Mission of the Catholic Church in the Nineteenth Century." Ph.D.

Dissertation, The Catholic University of America, Washington, D.C., 1989.

Quinn, John F. "Three Cheers for the Abolitionist Pope!" American Reaction to Gregory XVI's Condemnation of the Slave Trade, 1840-1860." *Catholic Historical Review* 90, no. 1 (January 2004): 67 – 93.

Raboteau, Albert J. "Relating Race and Religion: Four Historical Models." In *Uncommon Faithfulness: The Black Catholic Experience.* Edited by M. Shawn Copeland, with LaReine-Marie Mosely and Albert J. Raboteau. Maryknoll, New York: Orbis Books, 2008.

Roberts, J. Deotis. *Black Theology in Dialogue.* Philadelphia: The Westminster Press, 1987.

Rouson, Vivian. *"Waiting for My Church to Live Its Creed."* National Catholic Reporter 33 (April 25, 1997), 13.

-----. "Black Catholics Share Pride, Renew Roots." *National Catholic Reporter*, 33: 8-9 (September 19, 1997).

Schuster, George and Robert M. Kearns. *Statistical Profile of Black Catholics, with foreword by Bernard Quinn.* Washington, DC: Josephite Pastoral Center, 1976.

Secretariat for Black Catholics, National Conference of Catholic Bishops. *Many Rains Ago: A Historical and Theological Reflection on the Role of the Episcopate in the Evangelization of African American Catholics.* Washington, D.C.: United States Catholic Conference, Inc., 1990.

The American Catholic Tradition. *Three Catholic Afro-American Congresses.* New York: Arno Press, 1978.

The National Black Catholic Congress, "National Black Catholic Congress IX" (August 29-September 1, 2002), http://www.nbccongress.org/aboutus/nbcc-congresses/congress-09-PRINCIPAL-SPIRITUALITY.asp (accessed December 11, 2008).

Townes, Emilie M. *Womanist Ethics and Cultural Production of Evil.* New York: Palgrave Macmillan, 2006.

United States Catholic Conference of Catholic Bishops. "Brothers and Sisters to US." U.S. Catholic Bishops Pastoral Letter on Racism, 1979. Online at http://www.osjspm.org/majordoc_us_bishops_statement_brot hers_... (accessed May 4, 2008).

What We Have Seen and Heard: A Pastoral Letter on Evangelization from the Black Bishops of the United States," September 9, 1984, http://www.aodonline.org/NR/rdonlyres/ebfo6w4jkisjdpklqtq bk6euq7dzfrpnh7u7kpdapps6wjtyqepxjtnubgtwzvaqhxjlmtf22 rlmpctcgkwnrlfjicg/seenandheard.pdf (accessed December 11, 2008).

Williams, Eric. *Capitalism and Slavery.* New York: Russell and Russell, 1944.

Wright, Frederick D. "Black Liberation and the Catholic Church: The Louisiana Experience." *Journal of the Interdenominational Theological Center* 13, no. 1 (Fall 1985): 61-75.

THEA'S SONG: THE LIFE OF THEA BOWMAN by *Charlene Smith, F.S.P.A. and John Feister.* Pp. xvi + 319. Orbis Books, Maryknoll, New York. 2009. $28.00. ISBN: 978-1570758683 (paper).

Thea's Song is clearly a labor of love. The authors, one a member of her religious order, write in meticulous detail about the life and early death of this woman whom so many called friend and mentor. Their access to Sr. Thea's family, school, and religious order records enabled them to develop and present a picture of this intense and vivacious woman's contributions to her Church and to the world around her.

The work begins with the birth of Bertha Bowman, a long awaited child. Named after her aunt Bertha, Sr. Thea admits to having never really liked the name and used her nickname of "Birdie" more frequently until she chose the name of Thea (of God) at her first profession of vows. Born into a family that was both Episcopalian (mother) and Methodist (father), she was immediately exposed to cross-denominational life in the church, something that was a common part of life in the Black community of the 1950's and '60's. She was the daughter of a medical doctor (father) and teacher (mother) so was from infancy primed to succeed in whatever task she or others set for her.

The book goes into significant detail on Thea's early life, her introduction to Catholicism as a result of attending Holy Child Jesus School in her hometown of Canton, Mississippi; her introduction as well to what it meant to be a person of African ancestry in the pre-Civil Rights South. We follow her from birth through elementary school and witness her conversion experience as it propels her to leave all that she knows and loves in the Black Canton community to journey to the cold, predominantly white town of Lacrosse, Wisconsin where she takes up the role of aspirant to the Franciscan Sisters of Perpetual Adoration. She is the first African American woman to enter the order. In learning of her journey, we learn also of the journey of other African American women, who were also firsts in their respective communities. Their experiences reveal sadly that racism was not just a sickness external to the Catholic Church but was very much a part of it. For Bertha, soon to be Sr. Thea, this was a challenge. She was firmly convinced of God's love for her and all of humanity and saw no room for bias of any kind either in or outside of her church. This was an issue she challenged for the rest of her life.

Thea's rapid progress towards profession in the F.S.P.A.s was temporarily sidelined by a case of tuberculosis. Her indomitable spirit and optimistic outlook enabled her to persevere despite almost a year of imposed rest in a sanatorium. Returning to her studies, both religious and secular, she forged ahead into college and the postulancy. While working on her BA degree, Thea, like her sisters, also taught in the elementary school run by the F.S.P.A.'s. Her eagerness and love of learning soon converted all of her students and their parents as well, who were at first shocked and somewhat uncertain about a black religious. Their doubts were quickly removed and she became one of the most popular teachers at the school.

After her first profession, she was able to return home to Canton to teach at her alma mater and taught there for a number of years while spending summers first at Viterbo College and then at the Catholic University of America where, in 1972, she earned a Doctorate in English. Even there, her love of singing and dance, which had been somewhat stifled but never stilled during her early years in the F.S.P.A. manifested themselves as well as her wealth of knowledge about Black literature and music. She was asked to create and teach a course in Black literature, the first of its kind at Catholic University.

The authors ably lay out the trajectory of Thea's life post achieving her doctorate and discuss the way in which she was able to challenge the Catholic Church in all of its members (Bishops to laity) for its failures to live up to its own teachings on social justice. Sr. Thea was a founding member of the National Black Catholic Sisters Conference and the Institute for Black Catholic

Studies at Xavier University. She was a much sought-after speaker on issues and concerns of the Black Catholic community and the Black community as a whole as well as a world-renowned lecturer on multiculturalism, Black literature and Black music. The author lays out the trajectory of this shooting star, who blazed into life in 1937 and, too soon, blazed out again in 1990. But in the course of the 50+ years of her life, Bertha (now Sr. Thea) Bowman had a profound impact on the world around her. Taught from birth that nothing was too impossible for her to achieve, she passed that message on to everyone with whom she came into contact. Despite the rigors and pain of treatments for the cancer that ravaged her body, she continued to speak the truth to her people and challenged them to do likewise.

This book reveals the person behind the name, a woman determined to speak out on her faith regardless of the obstacles others attempted to put in her path. It leads us on an incredible and exciting journey through the life of this remarkable woman, challenging us to take up the staff of leadership that she once carried. The book enlightens, inspires, goads and moves the reader as we are amazed over and over by this woman who was an ardent worker in God's vineyard. At her death, she was acclaimed internationally and nationally as a true servant of God who "lived until she died" and whose legacy continues to live on in all of us.

DIANA HAYES
Department of Theology
Georgetown University
Washington, DC 20057

Book Reviews

RACIAL JUSTICE AND THE CATHOLIC CHURCH by *Bryan N. Massingale*. Pp. xvi + 224. Orbis Books, Maryknoll, New York. 2010. $26.00. ISBN: 978-1570757761 (paper).

Massingale's book should be required reading for every seminarian, priest, and Bishop in the United States. It is a cry of outraged love worthy of an Old Testament prophet. It is also a brilliant, lyrical piece of scholarship. Massingale, himself an African-American Catholic priest, offers in five chapters an insightful analysis of contemporary racism in the U.S. and the U.S. Catholic church, a history of the Church's few and inadequate responses to the problem, and takes the reader to a vision of hope and reconciliation. Thanks be to God for the latter, for at times reading this book I was so enraged at the inadequacies of the Church's response to the peculiarly American form of racism that I did not want to continue reading the book. Only the promise of a better, Godly response in the table of contents got me to keep turning the pages. If I had not, I would have missed the passion and holiness of Massingale's prescription for racial healing and Catholic engagement in fighting the terrible sin of racism that continues to metastasize in the Body of Christ.

The book opens with a clear and compelling analysis of contemporary American racism post-Obama. Too often pundits, people on the street, and our fellow Academics hold a shallow, naïve vision of racism as mere individual ill feelings to be treated as an individual character flaw. Those whites not personally prone to racial epithets protest that they are not racist, nor are any of their (white) friends, thus racism does not exist. If any racial disparities exist, they argue, they exist because blacks prefer to play the race card rather than to work. Yet, despite this blithe dismissal, reams of data document racial disparities in housing, health care, banking, education, you name it. For, as Massingale argues, racism thrives on an institutional structure put in place from the founding of this nation as a slave nation and codified legally through the Jim Crow era. This inertia of inequality did not disappear into the night after the struggles of the Civil Rights era removed racist laws from the books. African American lives remain marked by struggle, even as white lives are marked by privilege and entitlement (whether the latter are aware of it or not). Americans are raised in a culture of racism, which distributes benefits and burdens along lines of racial hierarchy: "racism is a communal and learned frame of reference that shapes identity, consciousness, and behavior—the way a social group understands its place and worth" (p. 25). Racialized identities form our identities and the symbols through which we navigate our cultural world. Thus much of the most damaging racism operates at a unconscious or subconscious level, shaping who we see as normal, good Americans, whom we want to live near, to teach our children, be our co-workers, our fellow parishioners, and our priests.

Sadly, this preconscious racial conditioning has shaped the leadership of the U.S. Catholic church as well. As Massingale amply documents in his second chapter, the U.S. Bishops' responses to the sin of racism have been lacking and issued only under pressure from Rome or from social upheaval in the U.S. The Bishops have followed, with reluctance, rather than leading the Christian fight against the evils of bigotry. Indeed, unlike Protestant churches with quickly responded to the 1954 Brown decision, the first U.S. Bishops' statement in 1958 came a full four years after the Supreme Court's decision and issues very little in the way of a call to action, recommending instead a "method of quiet conciliation" (cited p. 53). The statement did not even call for a desegregation of Catholic facilities or fraternal organizations, or condemn the violence directed at integration efforts. The Bishops' third and final effort, Brothers and Sisters to Us in 1979, pushed deeper in calling racism a sin, addressing institutional racism, and calling for personal, ecclesial, and societal action. However, as Massingale notes, the Church did very little to publicize the document. "Thus, many—if not most—Catholics were (and still are) unaware of the document's existence." (p. 67). One might steal a phrase from David Hume (describing his first book) and say the Bishop's statement fell stillborn from the press; and a study to mark the 25th anniversary of the statement found that very little has changed in the church's relationship with African Americans since its publication.

If St. Paul called us to be in the world and not of it, Massingale documents quite clearly that the American Catholic Church clearly reflects society's racism. Only a handful of Bishops have issued any statements condemning racism, few priests preach about racial justice or against racism, there is a paucity of black representation in church leadership at every level, few seminaries even discuss the history, culture and traditions of black Americans, only a third of dioceses even have an office for Black Ministry, and most of those are underfunded and marginalized. The majority of white Catholics do not appear to know or care about ongoing racism in society at large or in their own churches. The cultural meanings and values that maintain and defend a system of white social, material and economic privilege and disadvantage of persons of colors appears to have distorted even the house of God.

The picture here is both painful and ironic, because as Massingale explains, surely in the church if anywhere we possess a different set of symbols and meanings with which to defy the world's sinful ones. Human beings made in the image of God are free to resist and reject the world's seductive logic of power and domination. Christ Jesus came to free us from the sin and death, including the sin of racial hatred. The church is ideally suited to offer its counter-witness of love, "articulating a spirituality of racial resistance" (p. 85).The Catholic Christian narrative, with its alternative meanings and values of love, social justice, and commitment to God and neighbor can help free priest and parishioners alike from the myopia of white privilege. Catholic theological contributions to racial reconciliation are deafening in their silence: Massingale's voice is calling out to break that silence. He makes a powerful point with his insight that as racism is visceral and pre-cognitive, intellectual debate alone will not touch the sinful indifference of the white majority. Instead of rational analysis, he argues, racial reconciliation and justice require lament, "which both stems from and leads to deep compassion" (p. 105).

Lament bewails an evil reality, voices our outrage, pain and suffering and protests the horrors of injustice. And laments make up approximately one third of the Psalter and the majority of African American spirituals. Laments cry out to God in the face of brutality and suffering, yet proclaim that God will deliver. Laments are not mere catharsis, but speak a new creation of hope in God's ultimate justice. As Massingale describes this:

> Lament has the power to challenge the entrenched cultural beliefs that legitimate racial privilege. Lament makes visible the masked injustice hidden beneath the deep rationalization s of social life. It engages a level of human consciousness deeper than logical reason; its harrowing cries of distress indisputably announce: "All is not well!! Something is terribly wrong! Such things should not and must not be!" Laments thus propel us to new levels of truth-seeking as they raise profound and uncomfortable questions that cannot be easily answered with the existing cultural template. The standard accounts of social reality wither before a lament's strident account of agony (pp. 110-111).

This chapter, including sample laments and the call for laments of the privileged, moved me to tears. White Catholics (this writer included) must acknowledge and bemoan their complicity in the past and present exploitation of our brothers and sisters in Christ. How can we hope for absolution from God and our neighbor if we will not honestly confess? And how can the church offer an authentic witness if she, too, will not actively show contrition and sorrow in her own theology of lamentation? Lament can lead to compassion and solidarity with the victims of racism and energize building a godly human community. The Catholic Church could offer strength, courage and a faith-based narrative to those seeking to truly live into the baptismal promise of radical equality and to fight for bringing the kingdom of God's justice to earth. Only such a powerful counter narrative can overcome the radical evil of racism and white privilege. Massingale is offering the church a sketch of how to begin the battle.

Massingale's final two chapters flesh out the explicitly African American religious ethos of universal inclusion and equality of all before God. For those wondering how to begin picturing a church fellowship of racial reconciliation, the traditional Black (Negro) spirituals' image of the welcome table can spark their imaginations. The welcome table exists in the world where all, the most despised and outcast, are honored guests at Christ's table. The radical love and inclusion of Christ is the polar opposite of Jim Crow and racist discrimination. Likewise, the African American metaphor of the Beloved Community with freedom and justice for all, across color or nation or even religion, can help guide our struggles against racial supremacy's vision of white power. Real racial reconciliation is eating together, living together, and sharing power together. Massingale calls forth the meaning in African American communities' of visions---"visions spring form and fuel the nonrational centers of the human person form which come the courage, fortitude and determination needed to engage and persevere in protracted struggles against injustice. Only 'vision'—understood here as a passion or pathos—can lead to and ground effective justice praxis" (p. 143). Visions of the welcome table and the Beloved Community can fuel our hope in God's ultimate justice and give us the passion to try and bring the Kingdom here to earth.

Massingale closes with a final chapter on the role of the black catholic theologian. Like the black scholar, the black theologian must speak out for a community struggling against injustice. The black scholar must bring to bear his or her work on behalf of justice. The black theologian must do more: he must offer a vision of social change in the face of spiritual, political and cultural struggle. S/he must speak to a church trapped in the sins of the world and help guide her out of the wilderness---s/he must be a prophet of God's kingdom who helps the faith community reason critically on behalf of God's suffering people. "Our ultimate goal is to help transform the Catholic Christian community into a less imperfect witness to the broad, expansive, and inclusive 'welcome table' that is the reign of God. Our distinctive vocational challenge is to think through and struggle with the contradictions, paradoxes, and potentials of the Catholic faith, and then prophetically challenge this faith community's propensity to sinful attitudes and practices of exclusion" (p. 162).

Massingale's book is a model of that prophetic witness and a map for those of us who want to follow him on his journey.

SUSAN PEPPERS-BATES
Department of Philosophy
Stetson University
DeLand, FL 32723

ENFLESHING FREEDOM: BODY, RACE, AND BEING by *M. Shawn Copeland*. Pp. xii + 188. Fortress Press, Minneapolis, Minnesota, 2010. $20.00. ISBN: 978-0-8006-6274-5 (paper).

In M. Shawn Copeland's book, *Enfleshing Freedom*, the doctrine of the human person is explored from a new, refreshing, and eye-opening vantage point. Copeland frames the black female body as centerpiece for this doctrine, and interrogates the scriptural claim of inviolability and sacredness of the human person as applied to non-white, non-heterosexual persons in general, and to black women in particular.

Divided into five chapters with a brief introduction and epilogue, Copeland challenges her readers to consider the myriad ways in which bodies are marked by race, gender, sexuality, age, and class. Invoking the timeless wisdom of fourth century theologian and scholar Gregory of Nyssa, Copeland reminds us that the Body of Christ is represented by *all* members of the human family in every age, every culture, every race. "[T]he flesh of the church is the flesh of Christ in every age, ... is marked (as was his flesh) by race, sex, gender, sexuality, and culture" (p. 81).

Conceived as a work of theological anthropology, Copeland begins in her introduction by asking the question that all anthropologists ask: What does it mean to be human? More specifically, she asks what marks humanity has placed on the bodies of black women in particular. Their blackness and femaleness has de-humanized them in countless ways throughout history. These particular bodies, however, are at the core of fundamental Christian belief. Analogous to the suffering of Jesus, black women's suffering exposes our capacity for inhumanity, juxtaposed against God's capacity for love and compassion. Copeland's insightful discussion of the ways in which slavery, particularly the Trans-Atlantic slave trade, "calibrated values in core institutions" (p. 2), forces the reader to consider how and to what degree it modulates modern values. Indeed, one only need consider the suffering of the victims of Hurricane Katrina to understand.

In Chapter One, Copeland opens what cultural anthropologist Mary Douglas has termed the *social body* – the body as a symbol for one's level of entitlement (culturally controlled access to life-sustaining goods and services). Race, sex/gender, and sexuality shape – often distort – the entitlement of certain groups, and as a result those belonging to privileged groups possess the socially-sanctioned right to oppress and brutalize the members of less-entitled groups. Copeland then continues with a discussion of the creation of race-ideology, starting with the major thinkers of the European Enlightenment such as Hume, Cuvier, Kant, and Hegel, and their ideas of white European superiority over non-white, non-Europeans. Their racist ideas, their twisted logic of white-black duality (white = good; black = bad) shaped the academy for centuries and continues to do so. And in shaping the academy, they also shaped the social body, thereby creating a new way of viewing skin color as a horizon, i.e., a vantage point from which some are clearly visible and privileged, while others are rendered dangerously invisible. The writings of Franz Fanon, James Baldwin, and Paul Gilroy are among those Copeland uses to describe the social construction of beauty and goodness as the sole purview of whiteness, while within blackness lies ugliness, criminality, and sin – whites fall well within the skin-color, or the *white-bias* horizon. Our very humanity lies within this construction of beauty, with blacks falling outside the boundaries. In our struggle for authenticity, we must reject this warped social construction and see beyond the white-bias horizon.

Opening with Gregory of Nyssa's statement denouncing the institution of slavery as antithetical to the kingdom of God, Copeland reminds the reader in Chapter Two that the human body – the black body – is a basic human sacrament, and as such is a medium through which selfhood and freedom are realized. She then walks us through a brief history of racialized slavery in the United States, and the way in which enslavement was justified as being for the benefit of blacks. The slave trade was dehumanizing for all involved, not just for the slaves, but of all those touched, black women suffered above all. Copeland uses slave narratives to illustrate how black women's bodies were used as objects of property, objects of production, objects of reproduction, and objects of sexual violence. She then explores the concept of freedom – freeing the mind, the spirit, and the body. At this point Copeland turns to the fictional world of Toni Morrison to point out the ways in which slavery devalued motherhood and mother-love, and analyzes passages from the novel *Beloved*. This exercise reveals how bodies have been consumed by oppression and world domination, particularly poor black bodies, setting the stage expertly for the next chapter.

Chapter Three is a study of empire – empire as a force for oppression, the "virulent global persistence of racism, xenophobic reactions to 'illegal' or undocumented anti-bodies within the body of empire" (p. 57). Copeland characterizes Jesus' experience with empire (i.e., the *Pax Romana*) as one of the commoners, as a refugee. The desire for the Kingdom of God – the *basileia tou theou* – was in opposition to Roman empire and denounced Roman rule as oppressive. To those many thousands of poor, dispossessed commoners, Jesus was emancipator. In this chapter Copeland explores the ways in which Jesus' body is marked – marked by his ethnicity, by his sex and gender, and even by his sexuality. She discusses candidly the ways that Jesus' masculinity opposed socially constructed patterns of masculinity, thereby challenging the status quo. Globalization – the modern form of empire – is confronted here too, particularly the ways in which the new global system has created a hierarchy of race and gender. In this frightening new system, the darker one's skin, the poorer one's health is, the more likely one is to be poor, imprisoned, etc. Copeland confronts the way sex and sexuality are constructed and used in this new empire. The function of sex, she concludes, has been transformed into an action for the explicit use and pleasure of white male heterosexual privilege (p. 74). Copeland leaves no stone unturned here, as she challenges the Church's teachings on sex, homosexuality, and celibacy in a refreshingly straightforward and honest way. The Church's teaching on homosexuality as disorder, she says, is equivalent to its former teaching on blacks as inferior – a daring statement to be sure, and one that could not be more correct, more authentic, and more true. Finally, she states emphatically: *If Jesus of Nazareth ... cannot be an option for gays and lesbians, then he cannot be an option* (p. 78, emphasis in original).

In Chapter Four Copeland 'turns the subject.' She challenges the reader to consider carefully the consequences of giving in to empire thoughtlessly. Under empire, the subject is the conqueror, while the victims of conquest, the enslaved, become the voiceless objects of history. Copeland forces the reader to consider these victims as subjects. She unveils not just the physical marks of empire, but the psychic wounds as well – the internalized oppression, violence, and self-contempt. The centerpiece of this chapter is the story of a Somali woman by the name of Fatima Yusif. Yusif gave birth to a son, alone and unaided, on an Italian roadside in 1992 while onlookers jeered and insulted her. No one, apparently, attempted to help or comfort her. Yusif's blackness and poverty rendered her a helpless victim – invisible and hypervisible simultaneously. The pornographic gaze Copland alludes to in Chapter One's account of Saartjie Baartman in the early nineteenth century applies to the Yusif – these women's humanity is invisible. The pornographic gaze sees only their exotic inhumanity, the culturally constructed, socially-disentitled object of oppression. Only in solidarity with the poor and oppressed, by sharing their suffering and pain, can there be authentic healing.

In Chapter Five Copeland reveals the sin of racism, both ideology and practice, as in opposition to the message and meaning of the Eucharist. Racism infiltrates social, political, economic, and even religious institutions, thereby poisoning and corrupting all of society, including the racist. Copeland discusses the way that the slave trade wounded the culture of West Africans by casting the victims into a horrifying sort of living death. In this death, the victims became somehow commodified , their spirits transformed and trapped in the commercial goods for which they had been traded in Africa, thus twisting and warping even their concept of the supernatural. In the New World, the victims were stripped of their humanity and subjected to horrors "past telling" in the words of one former slave (p. 114). Following the Emancipation, the practice of lynching continued the systematic dehumanization of blacks. Copeland expands on the analogy between the Cross and the lynching tree. She finds Eucharistic solidarity to be the answer to the systematic devaluation and dehumanization of black bodies, and black female bodies in particular.

Copeland's *Enfleshing Freedom* is a brilliant, thought-provoking work. She engages very challenging ideas about the meaning of authentic love, solidarity, and the Eucharist. We Catholics, nearly all of us, were raised to think about the Body of Christ symbolically and dispassionately. Catholicism in particular is so rich in symbols and rituals that the real, the concrete can be obscured. Theology so often deals with the disembodied soul, thereby making the physical body barely relevant. Yet Copeland forces us to consider it physically, to realize that the Body of Christ is more than just a metaphor, and we, in fact, *are* that body. As Katie Cannon and Anthony Pinn point out in the *Foreword*, theological inquiry is shaped and enriched by placing the physical body at its center.

Unique, captivating, and dynamic, this reviewer enthusiastically recommends *Enfleshing Freedom* to all theologians who seek authentic truth. Copeland offers a fresh and essential lens through which to view the doctrine of the human body. On a personal level, I found Copeland's work difficult to put down, but also sometimes difficult to continue reading because of the harsh realities revealed therein. The section on lynching was especially difficult to finish. So graphic, so haunting, so ugly a truth – but so very imperative to try to understand and critique. Reminiscent of the *krypteia* of Sparta – the secret practices that Spartans used to terrorize their indigenous slave population, the helots – it was their secrecy that gave the Spartan masters much of their oppressive power. Like all truths, lynching – past and present-day – must be brought out into the light before we can begin to understand, deconstruct, and de-fuse its lingering evil.

Appropriate for graduate students, upper-level college students, and scholars, *Enfleshing Freedom* should be required reading for Theology graduate students, and absolutely needs to grace the libraries of all universities and colleges that boast a Theology, Religious Studies, Africana Studies, Multicultural Studies, Gender Studies, Anthropology, Justice, Philosophy, or Ethics program. It should also be included in the personal libraries of all serious scholars of these disciplines.

KIMBERLY FLINT-HAMILTON
Department of Sociology and Anthropology
Stetson University
DeLand, FL 32723

www.ingramcontent.com/pod-product-compliance
Lightning Source LLC
Chambersburg PA
CBHW071427160426
43195CB00013B/1838